# T·A·K·E C·O·N·T

# GRIEF
rebuilding your life after bereavement
Dr R. M. Youngson

## Books supplying expert information and practical guidance to help YOU take control

Titles published so far include

### ALCOHOLISM
insight into the addictive mind
Dr Clive Graymore

•

### DRUG ABUSE
the truth about today's drug scene
Tony Blaze Gosden

•

### FERTILITY
a guide to natural family planning
Dr Elizabeth Clubb and Jane Knight

•

### HEALTH DEFENCE
preserve and improve your health – naturally!
Dr Caroline Shreeve

•

### SCHIZOPHRENIA
a fresh approach to the subject
Gwen Howe

•

### STRESS
a new positive approach
Jenni Adams

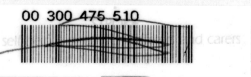

a self... ...d carers

EASTERN

# GRIEF
## rebuilding
## your life
## after bereavement

### Dr R. M. Youngson

**DAVID & CHARLES**
Newton Abbot · London

**British Library Cataloguing in Publication Data**

Youngson, R. M.
  Grief. – (Take control series).
  1. Bereaved persons. Grief. Self-help –
  Manuals
  I. Title    II. Series
  155.9'37

  ISBN 0-7153-9160-7

Printed in Great Britian
by Billings & Sons, Worcester
for David & Charles Publishers plc
Brunel House Newton Abbot Devon

# Contents

# Preface

Grief is the measure of your love and dependence and is the price you pay for loving. It is mainly a reaction to loss, or anticipated loss, but it also includes your distress on behalf of the person who has died, or who is dying. One of the things you need, right now, is a deeper understanding of both these parts of the grief reaction. For, with understanding will come some relief.

The period of bereavement is a time of great loneliness. You have lost your loved one, and now your friends and acquaintances avoid you. This is because death has become the great taboo of today, arousing fear, embarrassment and, in some people, instinctive rejection. Your grief, too, is hard for others to take and this keeps them away. So, at the very time when you most need sympathetic companionship, it is denied you; at the very time you most want to talk about the person you have lost, the subject is avoided in case you might be distressed by it. Even if you know that real mourning – the vocal expression of your pain and grief – is healthy and healing, you are expected to show no sign of it.

These damaging attitudes arise from widespread ignorance, perpetuated because no one will talk. This is sad, because much is now known about death, dying and the nature of mourning, that can comfort you. While this is so, nothing but further living – living, rather than time – can fully relieve your grief. So there is also much for you to know about this if you are to pull yourself up from what may seem to be the ruins of your life and return, once again, to some measure of happiness.

It is not going to be helpful to you if I deal with this difficult subject in a dry academic way. Even worse would be a sentimental or timid approach. So I have pulled no punches in facing up to the pain. From the pages of this book, many people, who have been interviewed, speak for themselves, telling you, directly, how it has been for them. I have changed hardly a word of these monologues. But as well as giving you these personal accounts, I have tried to bring out many of the central messages of the book by a deliberate use of the techniques of fiction. Although the events are real, all the names have been changed and often I have not hesitated to sketch in a new background so as to get across these important points more tellingly. I believe that truth can be conveyed very effectively by this means.

You have a long and distressful period ahead of you, but you are entitled to seek such relief as you can. The rebuilding of your shattered life will not be easy and you will need all the help you can get. It is my hope that in this book you will find something more than comfort.

R M Youngson

# Acknowledgements

Any writer of a book of this kind must be deeply indebted to original researchers such as Professor John Hinton, Dr. Colin Murray Parkes, Dr Elizabeth Kubler-Ross, Dame Cecily Saunders, Dr Richard Lamerton, and the late Lilly Pincus. The contribution made by these dedicated workers to our understanding of the subject, and to the relief of the distress of the dying and of the bereaved, is beyond computation.

I must acknowledge, too, the brave group of anonymous volunteers who, for the purposes of this book, willingly spoke of their pain and loss, and generously exposed their emotions, so that others, nearer to grief, might know that they were not alone. I am also most grateful to Elaine Mills, whose sensitive interviewing of these people brought out so much of value.

# 1 Preparation for Bereavement

A week or two before I began writing this book, I happened to be walking along a quiet shopping street – I had just posted a manuscript to an editor – when a heavy block of masonry fell from the facade of a building on the other side of the road. I heard the bang and saw the rising cloud of dust and walked across. A woman was lying on the sidewalk surrounded by pieces of broken masonry. Her right foot was hanging off and there was blood everywhere. It was a miracle that she had not been killed. For half an hour until the ambulance arrived, I supported her head and tried to comfort her. She was conscious and kept gripping my hand as if in great pain, but uttered no sound.

As I knelt by her and observed the damage caused to the car parked alongside, by the mass of falling rubble, it occurred to me that, had she been struck on the head, she would have known nothing of how her life had suddenly been brought to an end. Many deaths are like this and, in these cases it is only the bereaved who suffer.

For those left behind, such sudden deaths are the worst thing that can happen, for they are unprepared for the shock and the loss and for the many heavy responsibilities suddenly placed upon them. Perhaps you have been bereaved in this way and are still feeling stunned and helpless. If so, you have my especial sympathy, for the sudden death of a loved one is the most distressing of all, not only at the time, but for a very long time afterwards.

Many people who have ample opportunity to prepare themselves for bereavement, actually do nothing about it, so that when death comes, even after weeks or months of expectation, the distress is greater than it might have been. Many extra problems, which might have been resolved, now face the one left behind.

Either way, bereavement is agony. If you have enjoyed a very close relationship for a long time, you are going to feel as if you have been cut in half, and you will probably feel you want to die, too. If you have been married a long time, the death of your spouse is going to be like the cutting away of a prop you have been relying on for years, even if you have been hardly aware of it. You are going to go through a period of the greatest unhappiness you have ever experienced and it is going to make you fit for nothing. When the immediacy of agony passes, you will have to consider how you are going to live the rest of your life and how you are going to cope. You are going to think, endlessly, about the loved one you have lost and about whether you did your best. You are going to feel guilt, anger, depression, loneliness and despair. You are going to have many practical problems which you will feel totally unable to manage. It will be too late, then, to wish that you had considered some of these beforehand and sorted them out.

In the initial weeks of bereavement, you are going to have to be able to function with some sort of efficiency, even if you feel like a robot, and it will be as well if you have been able to organise your affairs in such a way that important things will happen automatically.

## PREPARATION

In most cases of serious illness, there is a period of warning, often a prolonged period, before death occurs, and this allows you time for such preparation. If your relationship is a good one, you will want to do this, and should not find it particularly difficult. A seriously ill man should, and usually will, want to set his mind at rest about the financial security of his wife, and a dying wife will want to tell her husband many things he will need to know when he is alone. To think it heartless to want to discuss such things is a complete misunderstanding. Such discussion can be conducted on a 'you never know what might happen' basis. Older couples with a good and close relationship do regularly talk about one or other being left, and such talk is healthy and realistic. It is also loving.

This brings to mind a story told by a lecturer about his mother, who was always nagging his father about making a will. One day he heard her say, 'Joe. Put down that paper. It's high time we talked about our deaths. Now listen, Joe. Whichever one of us dies first, I think I will go live in Florida'.

The situation is not so easy, and the discussion becomes less theoretical when it is apparent that one partner is likely to die in the fairly near future, but has not been told. In this case the urgency for detailed discussion is greater, for there is much to be done. However reluctant you may be to refer to it, there are important practical matters, concerning your own future, to consider. This is the time for you to find out where all the insurance papers and stock certificates are, to make or update your wills, to discover each other's real wishes for the future, perhaps to arrange joint bank accounts, confirm your title to the house, make financial adjustments like converting growth stocks into income bonds.

But, just as important, it is a time for you – the one who is to be left behind – to start preparing yourself for the experience of bereavement; to begin learning the difficult and important task of how to help the sick person to die, so that the guilt element in mourning may be reduced; to begin to prepare yourself for, and strengthen yourself against, the coming state of solitariness; and to prepare for the remoter future.

## Communication Difficulties

In very few cases do both partners know for a positive fact – or are willing to admit to each other that they know – that one of them is shortly to die. Even in those rare cases where such knowledge is completely out in the open, the dying person will not, until quite a late stage, fully accept the truth. This often makes any discussion of the matter, even between close and loving couples, more difficult, and so the matter is often avoided.

There are subjects many of us could discuss more easily with casual acquaintances, or even complete strangers, than with those close to us. One such subject is dying. This strange shyness arises because when we talk to our intimates, words take on a wider than literal meaning, and their significance is coloured by the relationship. Talk of death, between strangers, can be detached and philosophical, but the same conversation between a long-married couple, especially if one of them is seriously ill, will be full of extra meaning and implication.

Some people close their minds completely to any thoughts of death – either their own or those of their loved ones. This is a pity and, of course, makes discussion impossible. But many, fortunately, are ready to talk, if circumstances make this possible. In the course of my medical practice I have been repeatedly surprised at the willingness – even the eagerness – of the majority of those I have questioned, to talk to me about such things as their attitude to death. I know that the freedom with which these people talk to me does not necessarily imply a simi-lar freedom with each other when alone together, but, given a little encouragement, many couples will open up readily in the presence of a sympathetic third party.

## Should You Tell?

Once it is clear that there is no hope, doctors will almost always tell someone. Occasionally, they will tell the patient, but more often they will tell the spouse or a close relative. If you are such a one, if the doctor has told you that your loved one is going to die, but has said nothing positive to the sick person, you are caught in a dilemma.

You have to consider whether to do the conventional thing – say nothing, pretend that everything is all right – and lose the chance of making any kind of preparation for bereavement. Or whether you should, very carefully and kindly, bring the matter out into the open. I suggest that this is probably the right thing.

You may feel that it is going to be difficult or impossible for you to make this effort. You may question that it is the right thing to do – that the last thing in the world you want is to pass on this worst of all news to your loved one. You may be right. Every case is different. But have you really considered all the factors? Let's at least look at the main aspects of this important question – should you tell?

Almost all of those who are professionally concerned with the dying agree that, with careful reservations, it is better that the person concerned should know the truth. Concealment, which is the usual pattern, can have serious consequences, as we shall see, and there is ample evidence that, at some stage, those who are dying want to have the fact out in the open. But, of course, it is a very difficult thing to tell a person, or to imply, that he or she is shortly to die.

The decision is likely to be a very painful one, but you will find much in this book which will help you to make up your mind.

## Hope is Essential

The next chapter deals with the question of how to talk about death. Please note, however, that if, after reading this far, you do decide to tell, you should never, under any circumstances, come out with a bald statement, such as 'The doctor says you are going to die. There is no chance that you will recover.' Even if the dying person gives every indication of wanting to know, and seems ready to accept the final truth, you must never put the matter in such a way as to deny any hope of the possibility of recovery. Hope is a vital ingredient in maintaining reasonable peace of mind and one can almost always rely on a kind of self-deception, on the part of the patient, to make the most of the slim hope you leave.

William Osler, the great physician, whose influence on modern medicine has been profound, said: 'One thing is certain; it is not for you to don the black cap and, assuming the judicial function, take hope away from any patient.'

Osler was advising doctors on this matter, but the same applies to you, once you know the truth. How much is told, and how quickly, depends on your judgement of the dying person's ability to cope with the truth. You should also consider how important it would be to him, or her, to be able to discharge necessary legal and financial responsibilities. You may be aware that a will is out of date, or has not even been made. Things like religious belief may make a difference to the way you handle the situation.

Never try to force the truth on someone not ready to receive it. You will already have a fairly clear idea of how much is understood – in most cases, this will be more than you suspect – and, based on this, try to assess how much of the trust is really wanted. If your loved one says to you: 'Am I going to die?' you should not rush in and say 'Yes'. A question like this could be an indication that the dying person actually believes that the illness is fatal and wants to bring the matter out into the open; or it could merely be asked in the hope that you can give a reassuring denial. So your response should be to ask: 'What do you think, yourself?' The answer to this question may guide you on how to proceed.

Truth of this sort is always best conveyed by a quiet acceptance of the patient's own statements. You have to feel your way very carefully, making use of your opportunities to achieve shared knowledge. You should, if you can, select your time carefully. Be sure that the dying person will have plenty of company and support following the revelation. Once the matter is open for discussion, you must be honest about the probabilities, while remaining optimistic about the possibilities.

## The Relief of the Truth

All cases differ in detail, but they have much in common. This is what happened in the case of Michael and Frances Saunders.

They had been silent for many minutes, when Michael suddenly said, 'Do you think I'm going to die?'

Frances took a quick breath, intending, almost instinctively, to say 'No, of course not, darling,' but then stopped, aware at once of the significance conveyed by her momentary silence. She glanced at him with agonised concern, but the expression on his pale thin face did not change.

'What do you think?' he asked.

She gripped his hand. 'I couldn't bear that, love,' she said.

Weakly, he returned the pressure of her hand. 'John thinks so, I imagine,' he said, quietly.

She knew that he was offering her a lead, and suddenly all the agony and loneliness of the previous weeks swept over her and she was strongly tempted to take it. But, in spite of his calmness, she saw a hint of fear behind the expression of enquiry.

'He's a good doctor,' she said, 'He knows that one can never be absolutely sure.'

'Yes', he said, 'Of course'.

Frances looked at him, her face drawn with love and compassion. 'He thinks you should know', she said slowly, 'that this is a ... distinct possibility.'

Michael smiled a little, and then gave a deep sigh, and Frances thought there was more of relief in it than distress. He looked wistfully at her. 'I wish I could tell you how sorry I am to be leaving you.'

Frances gave a little cry and knelt down by the side of the bed.

'Now we can talk', he said, 'at last'.

Michael died two weeks later, and during that time Frances and he had rarely been apart. Once the barrier of pretence had been removed, a new element of grace had entered their relationship and they had talked more freely than they had ever done, sometimes almost cheerfully, about many things that were important to them both. After he died, Frances suffered terrible grief and, at first believed that the closeness of their last days together made the loss of him even harder to bear. But soon she came to see that nothing would have been worse than the loss of these precious and unrestrained insights into the depth of his feelings for her.

## The Absolute Veto

Often relatives find it impossible even to mention the possibility of death. Ironically, the patient, too, although sometimes aware of what is happening, will also often enter into the conspiracy and pretend that nothing is wrong. This can be comforting and will enable some to live through the most difficult period. But to maintain the fiction right up to the moment of death can be very damaging and undesirable. As we have seen, it is a matter of ordinary kindness and of carefully judging when the time is right to bring the truth out into the open. For most people there will come a time when honesty is deeply welcomed.

## Rejection of Truth

Melanie Wright was one who was denied the blessing of sharing the final truth with those closest to her.

When Paul was told that his wife was dying of widespread breast cancer, he at once shut his mind to what the surgeon had said, and refused to acknowledge it. Paul had never been able to express his feelings. When they had first met, he had dated Melanie for months, in a dead-pan sort of way, never showing, by word or action that he was interested. In fact, she was the only woman he had ever been attracted to and, almost from the beginning, he had been deeply devoted to her. It was only because of his persistence in dating her that she had had any idea that he cared and, in the end, it was she who had had to suggest marriage. Melanie had learned to take for granted his unexpressed feelings for her.

'You'll be as right as rain in a few weeks', he said to Melanie as he was driving her home from the Radiotherapy department, 'Don't worry. Everything is going to be OK'.

Melanie's sister and sister-in-law, who had, for many years, been on very friendly terms with her, were perfectly able to face the obvious facts, but both were exceptionally squeamish about disease and suffering and neither of them could contemplate discussing the matter with Melanie. Their response was to stay away and to see her as little as possible.

As the weeks passed, the evidence of Melanie's rapid loss of weight and progressive weakness made it harder and harder for Paul to sustain the fiction that she was all right, and soon she noticed that he was spending as little time as possible with her. Because they could not talk about it, Melanie was not sure why he was keeping away from her. She had no real idea of the seriousness of her condition and accepted Paul's assurance that the pain she was suffering – pain so severe that she regularly longed for death – would soon settle and all would be well.

Even after her second operation, which was followed by chemotherapy and radiotherapy, Paul continued to pretend that he believed she would recover. But the pretence was becoming increasingly difficult and he began to spend less time with her than usual. It did not occur to her that he was avoiding her because he could not face the evidence of her deteriorating condition.

'I suppose I'm not looking terribly attractive, these days', she said, wearily.

'I like you slim'. He tried to smile.

Melanie was deeply hurt by his neglect and apparent loss of affection. She loved him deeply and was desperately worried that, if they should drift apart, he would come to grief. She knew he needed someone stronger than himself, and was sure that, on his own, he would sink into a sorry state of idleness and unhappiness. But, in the circumstances, it was difficult for her to more than hint. Sometimes she tried to play on his sympathy.

'Maybe you won't have to put up with me much longer, Paul.'

'What do you mean?'

'You know what I mean. It's quite possible that I might not pull through . . .'

'Now, come on! You know that's nonsense! You're going to be all right. Everyone says so.'

Her eyes filled with tears. 'I know,' she said, 'By next year . . . But what's the point? It's not as if you cared!'

'Look Mel. I have to go. There's a smashing prospect in Clapham and I think I can swing a really big policy. Anything I can get you before I got out?'

'No. Nothing.' She turned slowly to face the wall, dragging the duvet across her shoulders. The pain in her spine was dreadful and she was not going to complain. And she had already had her day's ration of Pethidine.

'Good luck!' she said, hoarsely, as he went out.

Melanie had no idea that he was still deeply in love with her, for everything in his behaviour suggested that he had rejected her. Since the loss of her second breast and the thinning of her hair from the treatment she was convinced that she was no longer attractive to him and he was simply trying to be kind. Paul knew what she thought, but he was so terrified even to hint at the true state of affairs, that he could do nothing to reassure her. Towards the end, his conflict of emotion became almost too much for him and provoked a reaction bordering on cruelty.

'Mel', he said, 'If you can't pull yourself together and snap out of this depression, I'm going to leave you . . .'

The doctor visiting soon afterwards, found her in a state of hysterical despair. He listened to her for half an hour, gave her an injection and went out to talk to Paul.

'You couldn't stand by her for just a few weeks longer, I suppose?' he said, cuttingly, 'You won't have to bother for long . . .'

'It's the pretending . . .' said Paul, tears in his eyes. 'I can't keep it up.'

'Do you want me to tell her? Maybe it's time she knew.'

'No! Oh no! You mustn't. I won't allow it!'

The doctor did not insist and soon the situation deteriorated to the point where Paul hardly saw Melanie at all. He never stopped thinking about her and about what she meant to him, but employed a full-time nurse to look after her and she died alone and friendless, convinced that his love had turned to indifference.

## DYING IS A TIME FOR COMMUNICATION

The conspiracy of silence can have tragic consequences. Many people have secret regrets over cruel or unkind remarks they have made and for which they would like to apologise. Some may be oppressed by quarrels they want to make up, even wrongs they anxiously want to put right. Dying is a time for the removal of these barbs from the mind, but unless it is acknowledged that someone is dying, the licence to confession of this kind is not granted and death may be more bitter for it.

Many long-sustained quarrels are made up on the death-bed and ruinous misunderstandings resolved. It is common for people to spend hours with a dying person, discussing problems that have damaged relationships and blighted lives, only to find that the dislike and aggression had been based on misinterpretation and maintained by separation.

## SOCIAL ATTITUDES TO BEREAVEMENT

For all our claims to civilisation, it is apparent that our attitudes to death are less healthy, and cause more pain and distress than those of many simpler peoples. We have rejected the truth that death is a part of life, that there is a time to die and a time when it is good to die. In my younger days, I have heard older and wiser doctors talk of 'a good death'. Now I think I understand what they meant – a death of quiet dignity, peace and acceptance, at the proper time, surrounded by loving friends and relatives.

But, even today, few of us seem to understand these things. We want to hide death away, to pretend that it doesn't happen. There are priests who are uneasy and unhelpful in the presence of death, doctors who cannot face what seems to them to be their failure, nurses who walk past the door of the room of the dying person. We avoid the dying, lie to them about their condition, visit them but cannot talk to them, deny them the right to this great moment of their lives. And when they do die, we employ cosmeticians to make them look as if they are still alive.

This is a denial of the truth. There is little comfort in it for the truly bereaved – for those closest to the dying person who must, both before and after the death, conceal their grief from the dying person and from everyone else. Primitive death rituals may seem strange, sometimes even savage, but the dying person acquires great respect and the free release of emotion is healthy and natural.

## The Pioneers

Happily, there is a strong and growing movement to change our current social attitudes to death, and this has been the work of a comparatively small group of dedicated people. Dr Elizabeth Kubler-Ross's book *On Death and Dying* has become a classic and is required reading for anyone taking a professional interest in the subject. But she is by no means the only pioneer. In Britain, Dr Cecily Saunders' work to promote the hospice movement was recognised by a grateful government by the award of a title. Professor John Hinton, a noted psychiatrist, made a detailed study of the reactions of the dying and their relatives and, in 1967, published 'Dying', which has remained in print ever since.

Dr Colin Murray Parkes, also a psychiatrist, conducted a great deal of research into all aspects of the subject, both at the British Medical Research Council's Social Psychiatry Unit at the Maudsley Hospital, London and at the Laboratory of Community Psychiatry at Harvard Medical School, Boston. Dr Parkes worked in association with Cecily Saunders at St Christopher's Hospice to develop a system of care for families, both before and after bereavement, and did much to develop the major British organisation, CRUSE, now known as CRUSE – BEREAVEMENT CARE, for the support of the bereaved, which now has branches all over Britain.

Dr Parkes is now Chairman of the governing body of CRUSE – BEREAVEMENT CARE. His many article and books have brought him an international reputation. His book *Bereavement. Studies in Grief in Adult Life* is a scientific masterpiece, indispensable to all serious students.

## Preparation for Bereavement

The work of these people and others has shown that there is one overall principle in this – to know as much as possible, first about what bereavement is going to do to you, emotionally, physically, socially, financially, even sexually, and second, about the nature of dying and the feelings, emotions and fears of those facing death. Only by knowing these things can you prepare yourself for an experience that may prove to be the worst of your life. Knowledge is strength, and, in this context, often surprisingly comforting. You are going to need all the strength and comfort you can get, so I urge you to read on with close attention.

# 2 The Fear of Death

As we shall see, the final stage of dying is easy. The natural processes occurring in the brain, at that time, ensure that all of us may confidently look forward to peace and acceptance at the end. But most dying people have to pass through a period of weeks or months during which they are clearly aware of what is happening and have to face up to, and come to terms with, the knowledge that their lives will shortly be over. It is during this period that your loved one is going to experience the fear of death most strongly, and that you can be of the greatest help.

If you are to be able to do your best you need to know quite a lot about death and dying and this chapter and the next will tell you much that will be helpful.

The fear of death is natural but is seldom apparent unless death is imminent. Healthy people of all ages, of course, suffer acute and intense fear when face with sudden danger to life. At other times, the concern is so minor, especially with young people, that they often take terrible chances – with motor cycles, great heights, drugs, and so on, and the results are often tragic. The young person is unable to address the question seriously, and this is probably natural and healthy. In a study of attitudes to death in college students, over 90 per cent reported that they hardly ever considered death in relation to themselves. By contrast, studies of older people show that 60 to 70 per cent often do.

The situation is very different when the person concerned knows that death is coming soon. In this case, the younger ones, in general, fear death more keenly than older people. The very fact that they have been unable to think through the problem of death, makes the prospect even more horrifying. For the young and middle-aged, the approach of death is the ultimate crisis, beside which everything else fades into insignificance.

## Death in Old Age

Elderly people, especially the very old, are able to accept the fact much more readily than the young. This, too, is natural, and death is normal and right for people who have had lived out their natural life span. One does not necessarily die from disease or injury, but simply from the gradual ebbing of the biological vitality within the cells. At such a time, people die easily, without struggle or resentment and with an easy and accepting mind. Officious medical intervention to try to prolong such life, at all costs, can be inappropriate and meddlesome. If asked, the dying person would say, 'Just leave me to go quietly.'

Regrettably, we do not all die in this enviable way, and that is because many of us are cut off prematurely, often when life seems to be at its best.

## The Dying Want to Know

Many doctors and nurses when asked whether the dying want to know, will respond negatively. 'No! Patients don't want to know. It would be too upsetting. It would deprive them of hope and of the will to fight. And miracles do occasionally happen.'

This response may be as much for the protection of the doctor as the patient. Doctors wish to remain emotionally detached, and there is no way a doctor can maintain such detachment if he knows that the patient knows that he has failed and that death is inevitable. Many doctors fear the painful emotional outburst which they expect their disclosure would cause. They fear the distress they, too, would experience, and they fear the effect such a disclosure would have on their future relationship with the patient. Doctors have enormous demands on their time, but most are sensitive enough to recognise that if there is one thing that can't be hurried it is one's association with a person on whom one has imposed a death sentence.

With major advances in medical science, death has come to represent a defeat for the doctors. Many are conditioned, throughout their training and clinical experience, to avoid serious consideration of it. The constant association with the dying would normally force doctors and nurses to consider the inevitable fact of their own deaths and they have to find a way to avoid this. One way is by humour. Doubtless stockbrokers joke about a financial crash and I expect priests joke about hell and damnation. I can certainly confirm that doctors joke about death. And joking is, of course, a routine psychological ploy to avoid facing up to something.

Medical people have other ways of insulating themselves from these regular intimations of their own mortality, and doctors, especially male hospital doctors, often manage this skilfully. The physician dresses and acts so as to have distance from, and authority over, the patient. He uses language which he knows the patient will often fail to understand. He is master of the patient's environment and has complete control while the patient has little or none. This makes it almost impossible for any sort of real human relationship to exist between the patient and the average doctor, especially as many doctors think of their patients not as people, but as 'cases'.

'Sister, the Colostomy in bed 3 is getting a bit dehydrated. Press fluids, please. Oh, and the Stroke in 7 needs turning more often. Watch out for pressure sores.'

This kind of inhuman detachment is very common, but does not denote complete coldness of heart. It shows a deep need for insulation from the emotional effects of identification with patients, without which the doctor would have difficulty in doing the job.

It is an ironic commentary on the importance we place on money that the one argument that will usually succeed with doctors reluctant to agree to telling the patient, is that questions of wills or inheritance are involved. This is always given due weight and will almost always lead to agreement. Obviously it is important that people should be allowed to make provision for their relatives and be allowed the peace of mind of knowing that they have done so.

But there are many other matters which may be troubling dying people just as much. They may, for instance, wish to make up a quarrel or wish to apologise for something they regret. They may wish to disclose a long-held secret, or there may be some unfinished business or professional duty to discharge. Ernst Kris, a well-known psychoanalyst, after suffering a heart attack, spent the last hours of his life dictating to his wife important details about his patients which would be necessary to those who were to take over their care.

There are all sorts of reasons why many people would always want to know if they developed a fatal disease. Doctors are perfectly aware of this and will sometimes enquire of the relatives whether any such factors exist. But you may take it that doctors will, in general, try to prevent their patients from being told the truth, and some will even reject the suggestion that their patients have any rights in the matter. They will, of course, tell you, as a spouse or close relative, that they believe that death is coming soon, but most will not be too pleased if you immediately inform the dying person.

## The Conspiracy of Silence
It is certain that in many thousands of cases, everyone concerned, including the dying person, is perfectly well aware that death is approaching. Doctors and nurses, smiling confidently, calmly maintain the fiction that all is well; relatives and friends say 'Oh, you *are* looking better today!' and even get involved in a systematic pretence involving plans for the future. The patient, too, will participate in conspiracy, often because it is comforting, although recognised as a delusion, but frequently out of simple politeness. Dying people fully aware of the fact, will often join in the conspiracy so as not to embarrass others.

Surveys have shown that while about 80 per cent of doctors take the view that patients should not be told, about 80 per cent of patients actually want to know. Dying people, especially the elderly, often take a very realistic view of what is happening, and, more often than we realise, fully accept that they are dying and want others to acknowledge this too. Perhaps they want to talk about it. Perhaps they have questions they want to ask about the actual process of dying. In many cases, there are important matters they want to attend to. But, for many, the pressing need is simply to talk openly and calmly about the coming event.

Here is a case in point.

## The Comforting of Dr Lossow
Stanislas Lossow had had a successful academic career culminating in an assistant professorship in comparative religion. He was a quiet, unassertive man whose full power of mind had never been apparent until he was writing or lecturing. He had been respected by most of his students and admired by his colleagues and when his illness forced him to retire from the University he was sincerely missed.

Lossow had, for months, been slowly dying of widespread secondary cancer from a primary growth in his prostate gland. In spite of intensive surgical and medical treatment, the tumour had spread to his bones, liver and lungs and he was much too intelligent not to know what was happening. For weeks he had been in hospital, unable to go home because of one complication after another and he had finally concluded that he would probably never leave the hospital alive.

His wife Jeanette hated any form of unpleasantness and she consistently refused to acknowledge that there was anything seriously wrong with him. Whenever he seemed to be about to raise the matter, she quickly changed the subject and he was too kind to force the issue.

She was an attractive, lively woman, the daughter and sole heir of a wealthy wool wholesaler, and Lossow was actually uncertain in his mind whether or not she knew that he was dying.

'When they let you out,' she said, 'we are going to have a real good holiday. A sea voyage, I think. A bit of luxury and cosetting to get you on your feet again. Perhaps Greece, or maybe even the Far East. What do you say?'

Lossow took a careful breath so as not to induce the usual stab of pleuritic pain and said, 'Oh, that would be lovely!' and then coughed, holding a tissue to his mouth to catch the fine spray of blood, so that she would not see it. Because of her private fortune, he could not even bring up the subject of financial arrangements. His meagre savings would mean little to her.

'But I'm not sure,' he said hesitantly, 'that I'm ever going to come out –'

'Oh, what nonsense! Of course you'll come out!' Jeanette smiled brightly, 'You're looking so much better.' She took a quick glance at herself in the mirror in her bag and got up. 'I have to run, darling. Get well soon. See you in a day or two.' She gave him a peck on the cheek and was gone.

Lossow was in a single-bed side room with a pleasant outlook and received great kindness from all the medical and nursing staff who appreciated his patient tolerance and courage. Every day a stout, smiling Jamaican woman came in to polish the parquet floor and dust and tidy the room, and Lossow enjoyed her visits. She was always cheerful.

'Morning, doctor!' she said, one day. 'My ain't it a funny world! The doctor's in bed and the lay woman – don't get me wrong, now – is up an' doin'.'

Lossow smiled. 'Where did you get a word like that?' he asked.

The cleaner laughed delightedly. 'Thought that would make you jump, Dr L., but you ain't got no monopoly in term-in-ol-ogy.' It sounded like a calypso.

'So you're a lay woman, are you?'

She spread her fingers, and crouched back, wide-eyed in mock alarm. 'Ah better get out of here!' she cried, her eyes sparkling.

'Come on, now,' insisted Lossow, 'What's a lay woman'.

'Not what you think, man. It's the professions and the la-i-ty'.

'Quite right. But I'm not a medical doctor, you know.'

'Is that so? What kind of a doctor are you, then?'

'I'm a Doctor of Philosophy – a Ph.D. I used to teach in a University.'

'My, my! Tell me about it . . .'

Lossow soon came to look forward to Victoria's daily visits. He found he could talk to her about the matter that was never far from the centre of his thoughts.

'Doesn't it worry you,' he asked one day, 'to talk to a dying man?' He expected the usual denial response and was surprised.

'Who needs me most?' she replied, 'A guy who can do everything for himself? Or a guy, like you, who's havin' it all taken away from him?'

He was sure there were tears in her eyes and he was deeply moved, as much by her frank acknowledgement of his state as by her sympathy.

Victoria had had little opportunity to talk to a person of his background and spent so long in his room that the nurses complained she was neglecting her other work. So she began to visit him when she was going off duty or before starting work. Usually they talked a good deal, but sometimes she would simply come in and sit quietly with him, saying very little.

Lossow was very relaxed and open with her.

'Why do you do it? he asked, one day 'Sit with me'.

She took hold of his hand. 'Ah guess you need me.' she said quietly.

'Yes, it's a lonely business – dying.'

'You ain't on your own,' she said, 'Even when I'm not here, I'm rememberin' you.' She hesitated, then said, 'When it comes, you have to go into it all on your own. But, up till then ... you got one human being willin' to walk along the valley of the shadow with you.'

Later, she asked, 'Ain't you got no family?'

'No' he said, quietly, 'The War ... Poland ...'

There was a silence and he knew she was thinking about his wife.

'She's been good to me,' he said, 'We've been happy. This is too much for her.'

'Yes', she said.

He had a brief, uncharacteristic, moment of bitterness. 'She'll buy me an expensive funeral. A fine coffin ...'

'Oh, honey! Don't you fret'.

Often they talked about religion. Victoria was curious to know about the attitudes of a man who knew so much about the subject.

'Is it a comfort to you?' she asked.

'No. I'm not religious at all. When you know about many different religions it helps quite a lot with living, but it's no help with dying. I never could find simple, child-like faith. Pride, I suppose.

'Don't you believe in God, then?'

'I don't know what the word means. I have too much information on the subject.'

Victoria looked unhappy.

'Sorry,' he said, 'You must certainly not be influenced by me. Your faith is precious and has nothing to do with logic. Hang on to it. You're much more of a Christian than most of the priests I know.'

As his condition deteriorated, his wife seemed to find it harder and harder to visit him and she rejected, ever more strongly, the obvious fact that he was sinking. He understood this was a way of ensuring that she need not visit him very often.

When, eventually, the House Surgeon called her and told her that her husband would not last the night, Jeanette said, 'Is there anything, at all, that I can do?'

'I don't think so. Thank you.'

'Well, if you're sure ... Good night.'

Later, Sister rang Victoria who came in by taxi.

'Is he still ...?'

'He's conscious. Go on in.'

Lossow was propped up and so still that for a moment she thought she was too late. Then he opened his eyes and turned his head a little towards her. 'Thank you ...' he whispered, 'Thank you, for ...'

Victoria was weeping as she took him in her arms and her tears ran, regardless, over his pale, relaxed face. She said nothing and after a few minutes he smiled and died.

## Shared Knowledge

There is another important reason why denial of the truth can be dangerous. Human relationships must be based on honesty if they are to be secure and easy.

To go on acting a systematic lie over something as fundamental as the future existence of one of the partners in the relationship, it is bound to have a damaging effect.

In a symposium on the care of the dying, Dr Cecily Saunders, then Medical Director of St Christopher's Hospice, London, recalled how a patient had told her that for eighteen months after his first operation he was aware that something was wrong with his marriage but did not know what it was. When he had a recurrence of the disease, he asked for a direct statement from his doctor and was told the truth – which his wife had known all along. As a result, they were able to come together again and remained close thereafter.

Dr Saunders, now Dame Cecily, and Chairman of the Board at St Christopher's Hospice, emphasises the importance of the whole family, including children, visiting the dying person, so that the sense of family involvement is preserved. Children should, of course, be spared the sight of any pain and distress, and medical cooperation is essential. She has found that in the presence of death, long-standing family quarrels can be seen in their proper perspective and resolved.

### Facing the Truth and Acknowledging It

So one of the most difficult things you have to do, at the proper time, is to decide whether or not to break the conspiracy of silence and to acknowledge openly to your loved one that you know that he or she *is* dying. This act of courage and charity, can, in appropriate cases, confer much-needed dignity and comfort on the dying person and open the way to honest discussion which can be deeply comforting to the sufferer. If it is to be done at all – and only you can decide – it must not, of course, be done too soon. You must always discuss the matter with the doctor, and preferably, get the doctor's permission. In most cases, nothing should either be said or implied until active medical treatment, given in the hope of achieving recovery, has actually been abandoned.

But, although only those in medical charge can tell you whether there is any hope, and although they can advise you on the possible psychological effects on the dying person, the decision on this point finally rests with you. You know, better than anyone, whether your loved one would, like most people, want to know the truth. You may even know that the truth is already known, and just not being acknowledged. You may have guessed that your loved one is simply waiting for a word from you.

It may even be necessary for you to take on yourself the responsibility of ignoring the advice of the doctor. This is something you must consider very carefully and you are going to have to make a judgement about the doctor's qualification to advise you. When you do, bear in mind what I have said – that the whole of a doctor's concern, almost all of the time, is for the recovery of his patients and that to admit that a patient is dying is to admit failure. So you may also have to decide whether the doctor's judgement, in this matter, is as good as yours.

# HOW TO TELL

Even when all agree that your decision is right, it can seldom be an easy matter to tell someone they are soon to die. There are all sorts of reasons for this difficulty. At the beginning of an illness, and for some considerable time afterwards, one is, and should be, optimistic about the outcome. And even after optimism has faded, it is right and proper to keep up an attitude suggesting an expectation of recovery, and it is hard to abandon this attitude. Again, one may not be able to face the truth oneself, or feel that to say anything would be cruel.

It is extremely important, that you should never, under any circumstances, blurt out the bald truth of the matter. Never any such statement as, 'You have only a few days to live.' If you are to do it, you must do it by gentle inference and suggestion. You should, very carefully, allow the dying person to see that you know that the high probability is that death is near, but you must never say anything that will crush all hope. 'I'm afraid it looks bad, my dear ...' will often give the patient the chance to agree and to voice unspoken fears. Feel your way, gradually, so that you can assess what your loved one really wants. Some, especially the younger, will be completely unable to face the prospect and will deny that there is any question of a fatal illness. If this is the response, you must withhold your attempts, for the time is not yet right. Later, the response is likely to change.

The reaction to the awareness that death is coming will vary greatly with the mind of the person concerned and with other circumstances. Age, for instance, is an important factor. Elderly people, and especially the very old, often take the reasonable view that they have had their time, have lived a full life, and should not expect, or demand, much more. To them, the approach of death often seems natural and right and they may be much more concerned with the preservation of their dignity, calm and sense of orderliness, than with trying to prolong life.

To such sensible people, an unwarranted and unwanted medical interference with the natural stage, for which they are ready, may seem an outrageous infringement of their liberty. But, very often, being old, patient and tolerant, they say nothing. But this does not mean that they would not welcome the chance to express their opinion of what is being done. Maybe it is your responsibility to give your loved one the chance to speak, even if to do so means breaking the barrier of silence and acknowledging that death is near.

Old people often value their dignity and privacy above all things. Many have said that they do not fear death but that they fear the process of dying with its attendant intrusion of others into private affairs. This is one reason why it is nearly always better for an old person to die at home, in the presence of family members, rather than to die in hospital. The modern fragmentation of families and the abandonment of the old by the young, makes this a much rarer event than it used to be.

If you are going to make the courageous decision to tell the truth to your loved one, you should be aware of the probable consequences.

You know that death is likely in the near future and will almost certainly occur eventually, whether you tell or not. It will not be your fault – but the emotional reaction of your loved one, especially if young, may make you think that you have caused it. The background to our knowledge of these things is interesting.

## How the Mind Moves from Life to Acceptance of Death

In 1965, Dr Elizabeth Kubler-Ross, an American psychiatrist, working in Billings Hospital in Chicago, was approached by four theology students who asked her for help with a project on facing the crisis of death. They discussed the matter and decided that the best way to proceed was to interview dying patients. This was more easily said than done and doctor after doctor flatly refused to allow it. The response of the nurses, too, was antagonistic.

At last, Dr Kubler-Ross managed to get to a dying patient, an old man. He was obviously anxious to talk to her and asked her to sit down, there and then, and proceed. But she wanted to share the experience with her students and said she would come back the next day. When the little group arrived, the patient was having oxygen and was almost too weak to speak. He tried to lift his arm, whispered, 'Thank you for trying . . .' and died within the hour, unable to tell them what they so much wanted to hear.

In time Dr Kubler-Ross gained the confidence of the medical staff and, as they saw that no harm was being done, and appreciated the serious reasons for the study, more and more terminally ill patients became available for conversation. Soon patients were actually being referred by medical staff and social workers and, as patients talked amongst themselves, volunteers came forward. Dr Kubler-Ross made a practice of telling the patients that she wanted to learn from them what it was like to be seriously ill or dying. Many told her that they were very anxious to talk to her. It was often, she says, like opening the flood gates, and she learned much that she had not known before.

Among other things, she learned that gravely ill patients always knew when they were dying and often knew the day on which they were going to die. Many of the hundreds of patients she interviewed would, at the appropriate time, indicate that they knew they would not see her again. And usually they were right.

Interest in her activities grew and more and more students appeared to listen to the interviews and take part in the discussions which followed. In the end, these seminars evolved into an accredited course for medical and theological students, attended by up to fifty participants. From these hundreds of interviews she obtained much important information and established some basic principles. From this work, and that of others in the field, much is now known of the reactions of those told that they have a fatal disorder.

Dr Kubler-Ross found that, in most cases, the reaction came in five discernible stages. These reactions vary with the personality and, especially, with the age of the dying person. In young and middle-aged people they are particularly strongly marked. In the aged, they are much less apparent. These findings have now been widely confirmed by a great deal of observation and experience, and are universally accepted. The pioneering work of this excellent doctor has been an inspiration to many.

When we come to study the psychology of bereavement and the experience of grief you will find a curious similarity in the stages through which the bereaved person passes. This is not, on considera-tion, so surprising. Bereavement is loss, and the person who has been told that he or she is dying has to anticipate the greatest loss of all.

The stages are:

## 1 Denial
'I don't believe it! It's not true!' This reaction occurs even when the person concerned has guessed the truth and has gone to much trouble to confirm it. Denial is understandable. It is not likely that the habit of a life time can be reversed in a moment. All one's reactions are geared to continuation, to the forming and carrying out of plans, and it is very difficult to accept that this is no longer so.

The period of denial may be very short or very long. Some people have an amazing ability to weigh up evidence, to form firm conclu-sions and to face facts. For these people, the stage of denial may be very short indeed. They may simply say, 'Oh no!' remain silent for a moment, and then accept what has happened. But for most, the denial stage lasts much longer, sometimes for months.

In this stage there is much thinking to be done, but thinking is difficult for the mind stunned by such devastating news. Commonly there is a retreat into silence and isolation and the patient may refuse to see anyone.

You should not assume that the end of the stage of denial means that the person concerned has given up hope. Neither now nor during the later stages does this ever really happen. No one ever completely abandons the hope that there may have been some mistake, or that a cure will be found after all.

## 2 Anger

This is especially striking in the young who feel cheated of life and of their reasonable expectations of experiences of all kinds. Older people can look back on a life in which they have had a fair innings. The anger may be directed at particular persons – often the doctors or nurses, or relatives or friends who may seem to be getting an unfair advantage in life – or at institutions such as the medical profession as a whole.

All doctors are familiar with this effect. Because the anger has to be directed it is quite common for a member of the medical staff to be accused of some kind of neglect or action which has actually brought about the condition which is going to cause death. A very similar effect is, also common in the bereaved who also suffer powerful anger in proportion to the extent of the loss. You will naturally experience this, or may already have.

This anger can be very hard to take. Furious, cup-smashing anger cannot be kept up, but a slow, burning, intense hatred, directed against someone or something certainly can. You will know how your loved one tends to react when angered, but you may be unprepared for systematic nastiness, for constant carping criticism of everything you do or say, for dismissive ingratitude and for a total disregard of your feelings.

How are you to understand and learn to live with this? It is very difficult. You must constantly remind yourself that there is very little room in the mind of the sufferer for anything else but the intense feeling of resentment. In the circumstances, it would be a saint who would be able to consider other people's feelings.

The anger has to be let out and you can help to do this. Anger is rather like steam pressure rising in a closed vessel. If the patient is not allowed even to talk about the cause of the anger, the pressure will have to be released in some pointless, and perhaps more damaging, direction. Although it may not be apparent at the time, you will get much appreciation from the sufferer if you understand what is going on and actually encourage the direct expression of the bitterness and resentment.

Dr Kubler-Ross was not averse to taking a patient into her arms and saying, 'Why don't you just scream!' This might not always be appropriate, but there could hardly be more direct help with the release of anger than that.

## 3 Bargaining

'I will do anything, if only I don't have to die.' We have to be very understanding about bargaining, too. It is a kind of act of desperation involving a certain amount of dishonesty or childishness. 'I promise to be good, if you will let me off.'

People with religious convictions will try to bargain with God. To them, God clearly has the power to suspend the death sentence. Since one cannot live for ever, it is necessary to bargain for a certain period of extension of life.

'Just let me have one more month and then I don't care what happens.'

If such promises are followed by the desired extension, they must, of course, at the end of the time, be renewed. Patients will promise religious observances, a life dedicated to a church, a complete change of conduct, large donations to a charity – anything.

Some, who have not had any religious faith for years, will, in this moment of extremity, turn again to belief, but this is often so that they can bargain with God, rather than to have the comfort that they may, in some form, survive death.

A kind of unspoken bargaining with the doctors is common. Patients will often promise their bodies for 'medical research' after death, or will sign cards stating their wish to donate their corneas, kidneys or hearts for transplantation.

'You can have my eyes later, if you will do a better job on me and save me now.'

The form of the bargain can sometimes give a clue to hidden guilt feelings, which may be causing additional distress, and it may be possible for you to understand these and perhaps help to relieve them. For instance, there is the dying patient who said, 'Just let me have a little longer and I will forget the wrong Madge did me, and make it up with her.' She had not spoken to Madge for over twenty years and knew in her heart that the fault was as much hers as Madge's. She died, easily and at peace, soon after Madge was persuaded to visit her in hospital.

## 4 Depression
This is the saddest stage of all, for it is the stage of mourning. As will soon be clear, mourning is the response to loss of any kind and the greater the loss, the greater the mourning. However intense may be your sense of loss when your loved one dies, is this likely to be as great as the sense of loss for the remainder of one's own half-lived life? For the loss of everything one holds dear and of every friend and associate one has. For that is exactly what this stage is about.

Depression starts when the stages of denial and anger are past and when bargaining is obviously not going to work. It is a perfectly normal reaction and, however intense, must not be considered in any way a mental disorder. It is called 'reactive depression' and occurs as a response to loss.

This depression is probably the worst point of the experience of the approach of death, and it is hard for others to take, too. Weeping, by men as well as women, is a major feature of it, and this should not be thought childish. As in all forms of mourning, grieving is an essential stage in the process and has to be worked through, preferably in company. This is another reason why the conspiracy of silence can be so damaging. If one refuses to acknowledge that a person is dying, then it is, of course, impossible for us to share that person's grief at the loss of his or her life, and the dying person must grieve alone.

So we can, by courage and simple honesty, do much to help our loved one to pass through this terrible stage and reach the stage of –

### 5 Acceptance

Acceptance is different from giving up. Hope is never lost until the very last stages when it becomes irrelevant and is forgotten. Acceptance is a serene stage of readiness to accept death. The dying person no longer struggles against it, is ready to go and has lost all fear. This is the stage beyond words, in which human presence is wanted, but not for conversation. The stage of the quiet awareness of the presence of the beloved, the reassuring touch of the hand.

## THE DYING NEED US

In the studies and writings of all these devoted people, one central fact comes to the forefront again and again. The dying need close human contact. Nothing can substitute for that. One cannot buy what the dying need – only give it, personally.

Dying people need us desperately. They need to matter to us. They still need to feel important and to maintain their dignity while they are struggling with the terrible questions facing them. So our presence is essential to them. But we, too, when we are with them, are also forced to face these questions and, because few of us are willing to do so, we tend to avoid the dying, just when they need us most. It is only too easy for us to take the easy way, when we think we can get away with it.

Jeanette Lossow was unable to face up to the questions about herself that the sight of her dying husband raised. This is common and many people die terribly alone, even if their relatives are available to be with them. Stanislas Lossow was exceptionally fortunate to find genuine human warmth and empathy when he needed it most.

Much of the difficulty people have in facing this challenge is due to ignorance. For many, the taboo is complete, and that is the way they want it. But those who persist in this attitude are bound to deny their loved ones the help and support they need. So it is obviously important that the taboo should be overcome and if you have read this far you have made an excellent start in doing so. Knowledge can dispel fear, and it is my devoted hope that in this book you will find the knowledge you need.

# 3 The Experience of Dying

In bereavement, you have enough to do coping with your own loss. You have to work through the pain of this and you really do not need any additional burden. In this chapter I am going to try to relieve you of one additional pain you might otherwise suffer – the pain of contemplating what your beloved is going through during the last stages before death.

The patient's experience of these last stages have traditionally been described as the 'death agonies'. The truth is that the idea of 'death agonies' is a fiction, very convenient for writers of gothic romances or sentimental biography, but entirely without foundation.

The truth is different, and we have a great deal of evidence that the last stage of dying is, in fact, one of the easiest and least disturbing experiences of all. As it happens, I have some unusual personal experience in the matter, and I want you to have the benefit of it to help you to put aside at least this element in your grief.

## Acceptance is Natural

About thirty-five years ago when I was a young Army doctor, serving with a battalion in Malaya, I had an experience which I remember in detail to this day. The things I learned at that time have remained with me, all through the course of a varied clinical life.

Battalion headquarters, where I had my Medical Inspection Room, was an isolated area in Negri Sembilan and, because we were engaged in a war against the communist guerrillas, there were severe restrictions on movement. So when I was accidentally poisoned by an overdose of tetrachloroethylene, there was not much to be done. For three days I lay on my narrow bed in the Officers' Mess, visited at intervals by a very anxious MI Room sergeant.

My room was in an atap bashah – the walls and roof made of dusty woven nipa palm leaf thatching, and as I lay in that crude room, with the little gheko lizards rustling in the ceiling and the mosquitos whining round my net, I knew that I was dying.

I want to make the point that this was not a matter of my thinking that I might die, or that, in my medical judgement based on my own symptoms, I thought I was likely to die. No. I *knew*, with clear, unequivocal, conviction that I was dying.

Many times, during the course of these three days, I lapsed into unconsciousness and between the periods of coma I had a series of amazing hallucinations with distortion of space and time. But the important thing was that *I accepted the fact with perfect composure*. Each time I felt myself slipping into coma I believed that this was the end, and I accepted it easily. There was no struggle. No attempt to hang on to life. No horror. No pain or sense of loss. No regret for the loss of my life. Just complete acceptance.

I thought of my young wife and recently born child back in England and was sorry that I would not see them again, but even this regret was mild and passing. I was twenty-five years old, just at the beginning of my medical career. One might have expected bitterness or resentment at having to die so young. But there was nothing of that. Just calm and easy acceptance.

Later, of course, when I was recovering, I saw, to my intense surprise, that I had been mistaken – that the conviction was the result of an abnormal state of brain function, brought on by the depressant effect of the drug. Nevertheless, my response to that conviction at the time has, ever since, been a source of great consolation to me and I am convinced that, when I come to die, my last moments of consciousness will be as easy and as accepting. When brain function is dangerously dampened – as it is just before death, or as it is by a variety of poisons and drugs – two important things happen. There is a clear conviction of dying and there is no distress.

Since then I have learned much about the physiology of brain function and have studied the changes occurring during the final approach of death. I now know the reasons for the acceptance and easy resignation; but academic knowledge is one thing and direct experience is another and I believe that I have been extremely fortunate to have had prior personal experience of dying.

This is one of Nature's kindest provisions and we should consider it as normal. And it is a fact which I hope may be of comfort to those, like you, who must watch their loved ones approaching death. I am not, of course, suggesting that the whole process of dying is easy, and particularly not in young people. If there is early knowledge that death is coming soon, there is, as we have seen, a great deal of suffering. Nor am I saying that this alteration in brain function occurs a long time before the actual moment of death. That may be so, depending on the type of the illness from which the person is dying. Sometimes it does, so that for days or even weeks before death, there is peace of mind. But in most cases, this blessing comes fairly late.

## The Experience of Others

My personal observations of the deaths of others bears out this belief. There is also much support in the many recorded accounts of the deaths of celebrated people, to strengthen this conviction. People's deaths are as variable as their lives, except for this final easy period, which is common to all. Some come to the last stage suffering pain from the deadly disease, some remain in distress of mind until near the end. But all, at the last, come to death easily. Many drift imperceptibly into coma so that it is impossible to say exactly when awareness departed. Only a very small minority – about six per cent – are conscious shortly before death. A great many die after falling asleep in the normal way. Studies have shown that at least one third of dying people are unaware of their last day alive.

Michel de Montaigne, whose essays have entertained and comforted millions for four hundred years, describes in one of them what happened to him when he believed that he was dying from injuries.

'My life seemed to me to be holding on at the point of my lips; I closed my eyes to help me, as I thought, to thrust it out, and took a pleasure in my listlessness and indifference. It was an idea that floated only on the surface of my soul, as weak and feeble as everything else; but in truth not only free from distress, but attended by that tranquil feeling we have when we are gently gliding into sleep.

I believe that those whom we see faint with weakness in the agony of death are in the same state, and I think that we have no reason to pity them, and to imagine that they are tormented by grievous pangs and their minds weighed down by painful thoughts.'

William Hunter, a surgical and obstetrical pioneer with immense medical experience, said on his deathbed, 'If I had strength enough to hold a pen, I would write how easy and pleasant a thing it is to die.' Hunter a successful and fashionable London doctor, world-famous and rich, left behind, apparently without regret, a life full of satisfactions and pleasure.

Sir William Osler, the great Canadian physician and one of the fathers of modern medicine, wrote in his book *Science and Immortality*, that he could hardly remember a dying patient who, at the last, was afraid of death. Osler, in a study of five hundred dying patients found that only eleven were afraid, during their last illness. Osler was writing at the turn of the century and it may be that the widespread religious faith of the time was a factor in producing this low incidence of anxiety. More recent studies suggest that in the stage of acceptance, fear or deep anxiety are now much commoner and that those with religious faith show least fear.

## Science Can Explain the Dying Experience

Many people who have come very close to death, but have been saved at the last moment, have recorded their experience and the most interesting thing about this is how closely their experiences correspond. Common to nearly all of them was a strong sense of peace, contentment and acceptance. About 40 per cent had a feeling of spiritual detachment from the body and about one quarter felt they were moving into an area of darkness. About 10 per cent then were convinced that they were passing on into an area of bright light.

Medical science is now able to give clear explanations for these experiences. The sense of tranquility comes from a decrease in the rate of neural activity in the brain – the same sort of thing that happens with tranquillizers, or when we are falling asleep – and this results from decreased blood supply to the brain. Next, some natural substances called 'endorphins' – they are morphine-like chemicals produced by the body itself – act increasingly on a part of the brain called the 'limbic system' to produce a feeling of happiness and of separation from the physical body. As the blood supply to the brain declines further, the part at the back responsible for vision is damped down and we 'enter the darkness'. Before this visual area ceases to function altogether, it may have a burst of abnormal activity causing a sensation of bright light. And, briefly, just before the brain blacks out altogether, abnormal activity in other areas may produce a strong hallucination of bodily movement.

This kind of experience must, in the past, have caused many people to attribute some religious or spiritual significance to what they have gone through – perhaps even to take it as a proof of life after death. Walking into the light and then ... When we pass into coma, we are not aware of the moment of passage. The idea that we 'black out', in any literal sense, while actually becoming unconscious is not true. The awareness of blackness is a conscious phenomenon and occurs a significant time *before* we lose consciousness. We are *never* aware of the moment of loss of consciousness, and every night of our lives our experience proves it. So, if the brain is undergoing these progressive reductions in function, and has reached the stage of hallucination of bright light, we would then, if we are actually going to die, pass, without any awareness at all, into whatever follows. And there is no way we can ever know what does follow.

It is not in the nature of religion to reveal its secrets in this or any other way. If it could, these 'secrets' would be known to all and would be incorporated into science. Religion is, and must always be, based on faith in matters which can never be proved.

### Attitude of the Medical Profession

I wonder how many doctors take time off to consider what medicine is really all about. It is harder for them to do this than you may think, because they are intensely preoccupied with the purely technical difficulties of the job. With many good doctors, the central concern is the state of their knowledge. This concern is often competitive, forcing them to spend long hours reading medical journals and new text-books. With so much emphasis on physiology, biochemistry, pathology, immunology, genetics and so on, it is hardly surprising that there should be a tendency to neglect the human aspects of medicine and to forget that the whole purpose of medicine (and probably the whole purpose of life) is to promote the happiness of the human mind and to relieve its distress.

In my experience, doctors often forget that the practice of their profession is a means to this end, not an end in itself. I have occasionally asked doctors to define their function and the response has usually been – to know as much as possible so as to be able effectively to diagnose and treat illness. If pressed, any doctor would acknowledge that healing has a mental as well as a physical side and that their ultimate objective is the state of well-being of the *mind* of the patient. But in practice, this is often forgotten. Some doctors seem to consider death the final insult to their skill. Unable to accept the inevitable even when this stage is reached, they react to this situation by determining to do everything possible to promote recovery, at whatever cost, right to the very end. This is why we see people dying without dignity, in the apparent inhumanity and scientific coldness of intensive care wards, with tubes and monitoring leads connected everywhere.

The mature physician knows that, in every case, there is a time to recognise when his responsibility has changed. At that point, the doctor's duty is to look to the comfort of mind and body of his patient and to assist in bringing about an 'easeful death'. This couplet puts in a nutshell a matter which has caused endless heart-searching to many members of the medical profession:

*'Thou shalt not kill; but needst not strive*
*Officiously to keep alive.'*

Here is an example of a case in which this wise counsel was ignored.

## The Death of Nicholas Parsons

Nicholas Parsons was fifty-nine when he had his coronary. He had been a man of immense energy, intensely hard-working, a graphic designer, who loved his work above all things and had built up a highly lucrative business, with extensive advertising contracts, employing a dozen full-time illustrators and designers. He expected a lot from his team but, in spite of his age, would never ask of them anything he would not do himself. So as well as coping with all the administrative and financial responsibilities of the business, he would put in many hours every day at his drawing-board, a cigarette in the corner of his mouth and his eyes screwed up against the smoke, turning out the kind of brilliant work for which he was in such demand. His wife Caroline, who was twenty years his junior, would regularly complain about the hours he put in, in the office, but she did not really expect him to change his ways.

He had just handed a drawing to a client when it happened.

'Oh, that's lovely!' said the customer, taking in the bold originality of the concept. 'That's exactly the sort of thing I want!'

Nicholas mashed out his cigarette. His hand was trembling slightly and the sweat was just visible on his forehead. 'Good,' he said 'I thought the series might go on with ...' He stopped and began slowly to rub the centre of his chest through his T shirt.

There was a burning, gripping pain in his chest, passing right through to his back and down his left arm. It was the worst pain he had ever experienced in his life and he had a horrifying impression that he was going to die. He felt dizzy and faint and groped for a chair.

The next few hours were a confused nightmare of telephone calls, ambulance, Casualty Officer examination, electrocardiograms, drips, nurses, a ward bed, and then the relief of a morphine injection. When he woke the next day, the Consultant, Senior Registrar and Houseman were at his bedside.

'Good morning, Mr Parsons,' said the Houseman.

'Tell me about this case,' said the Consultant, without making eye contact with Nicholas. He was a tall, handsome, grey-haired man in a superbly cut dark suit. His shirt cuffs were stiff, snowy-white and there was a gleam of gold at his wrist as he stretched out his hand to feel Nicholas's pulse.

Nicholas, who was now feeling better, watched and listened intently.

'Mr Parsons came in yesterday afternoon with central chest pain, radiating down his left arm.'

'General condition?'

'Shocked. B.P. 92 over 40. Apprehensive, breathless, sweating, vomiting –'

'Cardiogram?'

'Elevated S-T segment V2 and V3 –'

'Enzymes?'

'Excuse me –' said Nicholas.

The two doctors turned to him in surprise. The Consultant looked at him, raised his eyebrows and said politely, 'Did you say something?'

Nicholas felt like an object, rather than a person. 'What has happened to me?' he asked.

'Don't you worry about that,' said the Consultant, 'Just let us do the worrying.'

This answer infuriated Nicholas. 'Look,' he said, 'It's my life you're talking about. Don't treat me like a child. I want to know what's happened. Presumably I've had a heart attack. Are you going to tell me how bad it is? Am I going to die?'

'We're all going to die,' said the Consultant, smugly.

Nicholas sat up in bed and pulled on the tube leading to a bottle of clear fluid high on a stand by his bedside.

'Careful!' said the Houseman, pushing him back.

'Better give him another 20 milligrams of Morphine,' said the Consultant and moved on to the next bed.

'I'll see you in a minute,' said the Houseman and then hurried after his chief.

Nicholas thought: 'Typical bloody reaction! Arrogant prig! This patient is being a nuisance – drug him into insensibility!'

But when the Consultant made his round the next morning, Nicholas, had decided to be conciliatory, and said, 'Sorry I was rude, yesterday. Just fright, you understand.'

The Consultant smiled. 'And how are we feeling today?' he asked.

'Well, I don't know how you are feeling,' said Nicholas, 'but I'm feeling distinctly underinformed. No one will tell me anything. It seems that you are the only person who can authorise transmission of simple fact. So would you be so kind as to tell me what has happened to me? I understand I have a legal right to know.'

The Consultant stiffened. 'Ah! A legal right, is it? Very well. Never let it be said that I deprived anyone of their legal rights. You've had a myocardial infarction.'

There was a silence as Nicholas digested this. Then he said, 'What's that?'

'A coronary thrombosis. Blockage of an artery in your heart. Part of the muscular wall of the heart has died.'

'Am I going to recover? I mean, will I die?'

'Nothing is certain. But with any luck you might pull through.'

'Might? What chances do you give me? Fifty-fifty?'

The Consultant shrugged, but said nothing.

'I have to know, I have a wife ... two kids. There are arrangements to be made ...' His mind was racing. He thought of his work, his business, how his family would be placed if he ...'

'I can promise you,' said the Consultant, 'that everything possible will be done.'

He moved on to the next bed.

Nicholas's wife, almost distracted with worry, visited him every day. She was no more successful than he was in getting a prognosis from the Consultant and eventually decided that he was incapable of relating to patients as human beings. Ready to go to any lengths in defence of her husband, she made discreet enquiries in the hospital and discovered that the Consultant was regarded as one of the most brilliant and conscientious men on the staff. Somewhat reassured, she decided that he probably knew what was best for Nicholas.

After several days of steady recovery, Nicholas, too, began to feel that the Consultant's attitude was probably reasonable. He had had some conversation with the Senior Registrar and had learned that in myocardial infarction there was always some death of heart muscle, but that firm healing, by scar tissue was quite common.

The evening before Nicholas was due to leave hospital, his wife had a phone call.

'Mrs Parsons? It's Dr Patel. I think you should come right away.'

'What? Oh God! What's happened?'

'It's Mr Parsons. I'm afraid he's had another coronary ...'

Nicholas was aware of what was happening, and knew, and accepted, that he was dying. He was so weak that he could barely move an arm and he knew, in a general sort of way, that although he was breathing as fast as his body would allow, it wasn't fast enough. There was very little pain, but he had an occasional fluttering sensation in his chest.

The Senior Registrar had been very kind and, although he said very little, Nicholas could read concern and sympathy in his manner and tone.

In the Sister's room, the Consultant ran the cardiogram strip slowly through his fingers, then looked up. 'O.K. What have you done?'

'Well, morphine . . . that's all.'

The Consultant stared at him. 'Why aren't you treating him?' His tone was chilling, disapproving.

'Parsons is dying and he knows it. There's hardly any functional heart tissue left. I think he should be allowed to die in peace and dignity. He's nearly sixty.'

'Oh, you do, do you? Well you get right through there and start the oxygen. And the Heparin. And the Lignocaine. And the Nitroprusside.'

The Registrar looked at him, but did not move.

'If you feel this way,' said the Consultant, 'why did you bother to call me in?'

'I know your rules, and I believe in conforming to them. But I don't believe in treating dying people as intellectual exercises. They have rights, too.'

The Consultant went through to the ward and across to the high bed on which Nicholas was lying, stripped to the waist, and stood for a moment feeling his pulse and watching the ECG monitor. Nicholas turned his head slowly and looked at him. The Consultant picked up a stethoscope and listened briefly to Nicholas's heart. Then he stood thoughtful for a moment staring at him before walking out of the ward. His Registrar followed him into the side room. The Consultant turned to him.

'I agree with your prognosis,' he said.

'Then we'll leave him alone?'

'No. We'll do everything possible. Just get through there and get on with it.'

As he was going back, the Registrar saw Mrs Parsons coming along the corridor.

'How is he?' asked Caroline, breathlessly.

'Why don't you come in and see him?' said the doctor.

They went in quietly and Mrs Parsons stood for a moment looking at her husband, then bent and kissed him. 'Oh God!' she whispered to herself. She was deathly pale and fighting to suppress her sobs.

Nicholas opened his eyes and looked at her. He tried to smile.

'She said, 'Hello, darling, how are you?'

His lips moved and he silently articulated the word 'Fine'.

Then his eyes closed again and his breathing slowed and seemed to stop.

His wife breathed in sharply. 'Oh no!' she said, beginning to weep.

The Registrar took hold of her arm. 'I'm sorry, there are some things I have to do ... some treatment ...'

She looked at him, hope springing up wildly in her eyes. 'You mean – you can save him?'

The Registrar was silent.

'Oh, tell me,' she pleaded, 'is there any chance?'

'I – I don't know. We must try.'

'Oh yes! You must try everything you can!' Her voice broke and she put her hand over her eyes. 'Do you want me to go out?'

'Please. If you would. You can wait in the relatives' lounge.' He glanced over to the nurses' station. 'Sister?'

Caroline went out with Sister and the Registrar wheeled the drugs trolley across to Nicholas's bed and began to inject Procaine into the plastic tubing of the drip running into Nicholas's arm.

During the night, Sister called the Registrar and he came down with a white coat over his pyjamas. One glance at the ECG was enough to tell him that Nicholas's heart was close to arrest. Dr Patel was there and had pushed the defibrillator trolley close to the bed. He had set up a second drip, running into Nicholas's other arm. Soon after the Registrar arrived, the electrocardiogram suddenly changed to an even, quivering, straight line.

'Ventricular fibrillation!' said Patel and switched on the defibrillator. He gave Nicholas a sharp thump in the middle of his chest.

Mrs Parsons came tentatively into the ward, but neither of the doctors saw her.

'It's a waste of time,' said the Registrar, 'Leave him.'

'Can't do harm,' said Patel. 'Nothing to lose.'

Caroline came to the bedside. 'What's happened?'

'I'm afraid he's had a cardiac arrest. It's what I expected. I'm very sorry. I'm afraid there's no hope.'

'What about defibrillation?' said Patel.

'Yes,' said Caroline, frantically, 'I heard what you said. Why don't you do it?'

Patel pressed the two round, flat electrodes to Nicholas's chest and thumbed the button. Nicholas's body gave a great jerk and arched upwards. Caroline screamed. Nicholas fell back and the two doctors turned to look at the electrocardiogram.

'My God!' said the Registrar in astonishment. Patel smiled.

'What is it?' cried Caroline.

'Heart is beating regularly,' said Patel.

'Oh, thank God! Thank God!'

'I think you should try to sleep, now' said the Registrar.

Caroline touched her husband's face and his mouth twitched a little. Suddenly, unexpectedly, he spoke. His voice was very quiet but perfectly audible.

'I want to die.' he said.

There was no resignation or regret in his tone. It was a simple quiet statement and deeply impressive.

Caroline cried out, 'Oh no!' but there was no further response from her husband.

Nicholas was still alive the next morning. When the Consultant came round he looked at the monitor and pursed his lips. Nicholas's skin had a bluish tinge and his breathing, which was shallow, had a bubbling quality. The neck veins were swollen and all the tissues of his body were puffy and water-logged.

'There's no cardiac capacity left,' said the Senior Registrar.

'Yes,' said the Consultant as he passed on, 'He's in extreme failure.'

As he was leaving the Intensive Care unit, Sister who was watching the monitor cried out, 'Cardiac arrest!' and the two doctors turned back.

'Asystole', said the Registrar.

The Consultant banged Nicholas's chest with the side of his clenched fist and said to Sister, 'Intracardiac adrenaline, please, and an endotracheal tube. Sister hurried over with what he needed and he pushed the long needle vertically through between Nicholas's ribs on the left side, right into his heart, and injected the solution.

He looked at the Registrar. 'Well man,' he snapped, 'Get on with it!'

Reluctantly, the Registrar started external cardiac massage while the Consultant, using a laryngoscope, skilfully passed a wide-bore tube over Nicholas's tongue and down into his larynx. At once he connected an intermittent positive pressure oxygen supply and Nicholas's chest began to rise and fall regularly.

'Check the central venous line.' said the Consultant to Sister, then, looking round and seeing Mrs Parsons, 'Get her out of here!'

Caroline ignored him and came up to the bed. 'What's happening?' she asked, anxiously, 'Why are you pressing on his chest.'

'External pacemaker,' said the Consultant loudly, 'And Mrs Parsons – would you mind?'

'It isn't going to start again,' said the Registrar. 'I'm very –

sorry. There's really – nothing more – to be done.' He continued to press, with straight arms, one hand flat on Nicholas's chest and the other on top of it.

Caroline looked at her husband's body. Two tubes were running into one arm and one into the other. There was a blood-pressure cuff round one upper arm. A wide tube passed into the corner of his mouth, held in place by a bandage tied round his neck. This tube was connected to a machine on the side of the bed by a flexible black rubber pipe. A narrower tube ran into one nostril. Three discs were stuck on his chest with wires running from them to a monitor. From under the sheet, a tube ran to a urine bag hanging from the side of the bed.

'Stop it! Stop it! He wants to die.'

The Consultant turned to Sister, 'Get her out of here'. He said.

Sister took Caroline by the arm and tried to guide her to the door. 'Come along, dear,' she said kindly, 'There's nothing you can do!'

Caroline shook her off. 'I can see that my man is allowed to die in peace', she said, fiercely.

The Registrar stopped the cardiac massage, looked at the monitor, glanced at the Consultant and switched off the ventilator.

'You're right,' he said. 'Just wait outside for five minutes and then you can come in and be alone with him.'

Caroline went out sobbing and the Registrar, without looking at his boss, pulled out the drip needles, the tracheal and gastric tubes, and the catheters. While he was doing this, the Consultant walked out. Dr Patel and Sister exchanged glances.

When the Consultant had gone, Sister said, 'I think you did the right thing, Doctor.'

## Death with Dignity

There are many records of patients who, at this terminal stage have, by intensive medical efforts, been brought back, temporarily, to their former state of mind. Significantly, instead of being grateful, these patients are often reported to have resented these efforts.

In the early 1970s an article appeared in the News Bulletin of the American Association of Retired Persons, entitled, *Death with Dignity*. The article discussed whether people should be allowed to die in peace when there was no medical chance of recovery, or whether every medical resource should be tried to keep them alive at all costs. Two hundred and fifty people were prompted by the article to write in and express their views, and of these 215 were in support of death with dignity. Only 35 wanted everything possible to be done to prolong life. Many who wrote had been deeply distressed by the sight of their loved ones being subjected to intensive care.

Nicholas certainly suffered pain and distress in the early stages of his illness, but almost from the moment he was in medical hands, that pain and distress was relieved. It is very easy for experienced doctors to see to this, and to ensure that even before nature takes over, pain and distress of mind are relieved. And you can be sure that, at the times when the situation is most distressing to the onlooker – when all the medical equipment is most in evidence – *that is the very time when the distress to the patient is likely to be least.* For it is then that the illness has the greatest effect on the brain – blunting consciousness, promoting acceptance and making the prospect of death easiest.

Take comfort from this. If you have had to go through the pain of seeing your loved one under intensive care, remember that the distress is likely to be all on your side and that, in all probability, he or she is suffering nothing at all.

Let us leave the last word on this matter with the wise old comforter Montaigne.

'It is not without reason we are taught to take notice of our sleep for the resemblance it hath with death.

'How easily we pass from waking to sleeping; with how little interest we lose the knowledge of light and of ourselves. For, touching the instant or moment of the passage, it is not to be feared it should bring any travail or displeasure with it, forasmuch as we can have neither sense nor feeling . . .'

# 4 The Care of the Dying

This important subject is at last beginning to receive the recognition it deserves. The emphasis, in medical science, has always been on saving people from death, and this emphasis has been one of the main reasons for the neglect of this subject. In addition, doctors, like other people, have their problems in facing up to the inevitability of their own deaths – perhaps even, in some cases, they have greater difficulty than the layman – and this, too, has discouraged their interest in learning about the proper management of the dying.

Medical detachment, while being a way of protecting oneself from the unpleasant effect of emotional involvement, also has another important function – to preserve the doctor or nurse from loss of clinical judgement. Many a time, while experiencing difficulty during an operation, I have wished that I did not know the patient so well. The awareness that a patient knows one and has placed implicit trust in one's management of the case, is no great help to concentration when technical problems arise. A surgeon who has to operate on a patient for a condition likely to prove fatal will seldom wish to become too friendly. So these responses do not necessarily imply that doctors and nurses are as terribly insensitive to the gravely ill and the dying as they often seem. But it is probably true that the majority of doctors are less than adequately fitted for the job of looking after the dying properly, and that those concerned with curative medicine are not the right people to have the responsibility for looking after dying people.

Fortunately, the care of the dying is gradually becoming recognised as a speciality in its own right, and experience has now shown that this is a discipline calling for the highest personal qualities – qualities not necessarily found among the most academically brilliant – as well as advanced medical qualifications and skills. But this message, and the central facts about the care of the dying, are still not as widely understood as they should be. A survey on the quality of care given to the dying, which was published in the leading British medical journal, *The Lancet*, in 1984, showed that relatives resented the poor quality of care given in one quarter of the hospitals concerned.

Many family doctors admit that they are not good at controlling pain in people with incurable cancer and almost half agree that they find the emotional distress of relatives and dying patients very hard to take. There has, for some time, been a growing realisation that this, too, is a specialised area, calling for a new kind of expertise and requiring long experience. And now the attitudes of the medical and nursing professions are beginning to alter. An increasing number of doctors and nurses are dedicating themselves to it, and accepting, along with this dedication, the often painful duty of identifying with their patients.

## Where to Die

Medical advances, the prevalent attitude of the medical profession and social changes have resulted in more people dying in hospital than ever before. Traditionally, people died at home, in the presence of, and supported by, the other members of the family. At one time, almost everyone did so, and there was much to be said for this. The resulting close communication and support must have improved the quality of death for many. But today, dying at home is the exception rather than the rule. Families are fragmented and separated. Young people have grown up and gone off to live their own lives. Many old people are living alone. Often, close relatives, who would gladly undertake the responsibility, are themselves elderly and unable to cope with the additional demands of a dying person.

The best place to die is at home, with the support of the general practitioner and the district nurse and the constant attendance of as many members of the family as the dying person desires. If dying at home is impossible, movement to a hospice is greatly to be preferred to movement to a general hospital. For, as we shall see, hospice staff know all about the central importance of avoiding loneliness and isolation.

Certainly, dying at home may raise many problems, and some are insoluble, but whenever circumstances allow, admission to hospital, simply for the purpose of dying, should be avoided. The difficulties may be great. Some dying people make impossible demands and are unaware that they are impossible. Some will insist that all nursing is done by one particular person and will impose a draining physical effort on someone who may be barely able to cope. Others will be only too clearly aware of the stress they cannot help causing and will suffer disproportionately.

In spite of the difficulties, every effort should be made to keep dying people at home. To be moved, at a terminal stage, away from a familiar and loved environment, away from close friends, pets, gardens, associations, to a place of strangers who, however kind, cannot be expected to take more than a professional interest, is likely to add greatly to the distress of the dying. The loneliness of the dying can be terrible, especially for those who have no close relationships to sustain them and those from whom the truth has been concealed so that no proper conversation on important matters is possible. To leave home, aware that it may never be seen again, may, for some, be the worst thing that can happen.

## A Badly Handled Death

Here, in illustration, is part of an account of a mother's death. In reading it, you should make allowance for the effects of this woman's anger.

'The first I heard was that mother had gone into hospital for a lump in the breast and they'd given her a mastectomy without even telling her first. I thought that was outrageous. She went into deep shock after she came round. The operation was supposed to have been exploratory and no one had warned her that it might involve removing the entire breast. She signed a form, but it wasn't clear to her.'

'She was an old-fashioned lady and didn't like having the intimate parts of her body interfered with. She had no help or sympathy from the medical profession at all – one of the nurses just said, "You've got nothing to worry about dear – they're only little ones anyway!" That was the attitude. I was appalled. She really had no decent medical treatment from then on until her death seven years later. They didn't bother to investigate the lymph glands under her arm. So then in six or nine months, they came up and she had to have the lymph gland operation.'

'After a while they told me, "Well, you know, she's got six months to live. And that's that." They said it quite cheerfully and matter-of-fact, as if they were talking about the price of bacon. They told me that the cancer had spread to her skeleton – it was in the hip and skull, and they said her brain would go at some time. They had more or less washed their hands of her at this stage. She was very low and in a bad way. She knew. She knew because the good effects of the radiation wore off and things started to grow again and she felt awful. She was prepared to go to a clinic in Mexico where they gave natural, raw food and used coffee enemas to detoxify the body. I don't know when she realised she was going to die . . .'

'I had found out about the Max Gerson raw vegetable and fruit diet – simple but it clears the body of toxins and backs up the immune system and it's very good. It's the sort of diet we should all be having anyway, low on fats and sugars, but minus a few things like – oh, I'm not sure – celery, I think, which helps cancer develop if you already have it, but which is perfectly OK otherwise. Every time I went I took the juices for her. She so liked it when I could do things like that for her. She liked the caring.

'After she started the Gerson diet she made incredible progress – in three months she changed so much. Her skin had been flaccid and yellow and it became alive and glowing. Her nails improved and she felt better. It was summer when they predicted death in six months. I put her on to the diet in September and by Christmas she was going for four mile walks. She had about three really good, healthy years, in a state of remission, because of the Gerson therapy. The X-rays showed nothing at all there – everything had disappeared and she was coming up to London, going to the theatre, going for long walks. She was careful and kept to her diet. She had to make these vegetable and fruit juices three or four times a day and she was well motivated because she was starting to feel so much better. To all intents and purposes, she was leading a normal life – and that was lovely! She lived for five years after they said she would die.'

'It was a great joy to go anywhere with her. She loved teas – naughty teas at Fortnum's. She loved ideas and was very stimulating. You didn't feel a generation gap. She would get something out of every experience. She was very beautiful – grey eyes, long hair, and a pointed Celtic chin, like Elizabeth Taylor. She was like the Venus of Boticelli's *Mars and Venus*.

'She had no help from my father. When they decided to move house, poor mother had to supervise all the packing herself. After the move she promptly had a relapse ... The move really knocked her back. At the same time my brother's wife went off with someone else. I think mother's stress level just went so high ... And father wouldn't help. She was eating junk food.'

'About a month after the move the cancer came back with a vengeance and she went back to hospital. When she went home she didn't have the strength to do anything and I went down to stay and help, but my father made it clear that I wasn't wanted. He was jealous and didn't want anyone else near her – he thought her loyalties would be divided. He didn't know how to relate to her and used to leave her lying on a sofa bed. He would take people through past her so that she felt like an object.

'She had another big dose of radiotherapy and more chemotherapy. By that time her skeleton was riddled with secondary cancer and she was very weak and not in a condition to diet. But she did have a semi-remission, and for about eighteen months was able to get around with a stick.

'Then Peter and I took a holiday we badly needed, and she suddenly had a terrible pain during the night. The doctor came and gave her too much morphine – in fact, poisoned her – so that when we came back she was in hospital – very confused – talking about things that went back fifty years or more. She had fallen out of bed and got horribly bruised. Obviously she was in mental anguish. She came out with some terrible things about her marriage. All the things she had been keeping down for so long were coming out. Terribly sad. That went on for two weeks after we got back. That was awful. She felt she had lost a month out of her life.

'She missed that month. She had an immense appreciation of life and didn't want to lose any of it. After she came to, she said, "Is is really April? There isn't much time left. I've lost a month of life and I would rather have had the pain, because then I could at least have looked at the trees and the sky and heard the birds."

'When she came home, she was very weak and ill. She was dying and she knew it. She said, "I do hope I'll see the Spring and the Summer." I said, "Mamma, the doctor says you might even see the Autumn." But she said, "Oh, no, I don't think I could. I don't think your father could bear that. He finds it difficult having me around like this. He's so impatient. I don't think he could bear me to live that long. I think it would be better if I died." She died two weeks after that – in April.

'The death itself was very badly handled. She had been at home and father couldn't manage. So he bundled her off to a hospice, annexed to a hospital. The staff and the medical care were lovely but my mother didn't like being in a group of four and having to watch other people die. She was terribly unhappy and constantly asked to go home. I think people should die at home, if possible, with the familiar things that they love and which anchor them to life.

'But my father said he couldn't have her at home. He said he had already got rid of the bed and had disposed of her wheel-chair. He didn't want to pay. The money was my mother's but he baulked at her having private treatment because it cost so much. Ironic, because long ago he had a brain tumour and she sent him to the London Clinic and paid for all that.

'He asked them to give her extra sleeping pills to keep her calm.

She said, "Oh, these are not my usual ones." I was there when she took them. Her last words were "I feel such despair. Good bye darling." She fell asleep and never recovered consciousness. That's not a death I would wish for anyone. In a way, they murdered her because it was convenient. She should have died peacefully at home – a peaceful, dignified, calm sort of death – a proper death-bed death. She should have been able to say goodbye properly and die properly – not in a drugged state – pain-killers perhaps – but not in a drugged coma.

'We were offered the choice of whether we wanted her to take the drugs or not, but they didn't really explain. If they had said, "Does she mind putting up with a certain amount of pain to preserve lucidity or would she prefer to have no pain and be slightly dull all the time?" we would have at least had an informed choice. When it comes to my turn we'll not use drugs at all.

Please note that it would be quite wrong to suppose that there is clear medical evidence that any kind of diet can modify or cure existing cancers.

### The Death of Bill Bratwell
In striking contrast, here is the touching story of the death of an old man.

Bill had been a fighter all his life and wasn't going to give in easily when the doctor told him he had cancer. He was widely admired for his courage and toughness and it had not occurred to the doctor to try to conceal the truth from him.

'I shall want you in hospital right away.'

'A operation, is it?'

'Afraid so.'

'Give me a noo stummick, will they?'

'Well ... no ... not really. But I'm afraid they're going to have to take away the one you have ...'

'Greedy barstards! I 'ope yer mates know wot they're abaht.'

'It's your only chance. You'll have to trust them.'

Bill shrugged. 'Wotever you say, doctor.'

In hospital, Bill was a great success with the medical staff and adored by the nurses. He was kept in rather longer than was really necessary and no one wanted to admit that his case was hopeless. But, at length the outcome became only too apparent. A second, palliative, operation, to relieve intestinal obstruction, was done and then it was decided that he should go home to die. Bill took the news of the inoperable state of his stomach cancer with characteristic laconic humour.

'ow long 'ave I got, then doctor?'

'With luck – six months.'

'Wiv' luck an' a bit of a barney, 'ow long?'

'Six months, Bill. I'm sorry.'

'Toss you, double or quits, doctor.'

Bill was the patriarch of a large family, scattered around the Woolwich area of East London – a family whose main activity appeared to be helping the police with their enquiries. When the news got around that he was dying, his sons, daughters, younger brothers, nephews, nieces, cousins, even grandchildren began to converge on the little house on the edge of Plumstead Common. The general feeling was one of outrage that the man they had regarded as immortal was dying.

'Dad,' said his eldest son, 'Nuffin but the best, fer you. Them National 'ealth quacks don' know their job. Leave it ter me.'

The next day Bill was driven to Harley Street to be examined by a private specialist. Unfortunately, the expense was wasted and, after reviewing the whole case, the distinguished consultant could only confirm, somewhat nervously, what the family had already been told.

Bill settled down at home and was soon confined to bed. The family doctor was active in his attendance, advice and liaison with the local authorities. Friends and neighbours rallied round, and there was no shortage of assistance.

As Bill began to have increasing pain from spread of tumour to the bones, there were regular visits from several members of the staff of a South London Hospice, who saw to his pain control and, talked to him about his condition and attitudes to death. In addition, an attractive young blonde lady, a clever and highly qualified social worker, went to see Bill every week.

What was extraordinary about Bill's case, however, was this. As he got worse and it became apparent that he did not have long to live, the family – all three generations – visited Plumstead more and more regularly and gradually took over the duties which were being performed by the various official visitors.

The blonde social worker was not received very graciously, but it was clear that Bill fancied her and she was grudgingly allowed access and would sit by his bed-side for an hour twice a week, holding his hand and often saying nothing at all. But, in the end, even she, along with all the others were turned away at the door as the family finally took over the whole conduct of the dying of their loved and respected head.

Bill, by now was having very little pain and, for that, his wife prescribed gin-and-water in liberal doses. Bill was allowed to eat anything he fancied, and during his last few days managed to put away many pints of draught Guinness and a fair quantity of the best jellied eels that love, devotion, and much searching could procure. Bill died smiling, surrounded by mourning relatives, pressing close to try to demonstrate their affection and concern.

It was weeks before all those gathered had dispersed and returned to normal activities, and during these weeks they talked about little besides Bill and the fine life that he had led. Over and over again, in various combinations, they met to talk about Bill and the many incidents, minor and important, of his long and greatly admired career. This was how they mourned him – directly, openly, frankly, unashamed of their grief and tears – remembering him, handing on their knowledge of his life and times to the young ones, giving him the respect they felt due to him, and the love.

## Using Available Services

Some people with fatal illnesses would suffer severe pain and distress without constant skilled medical attention, but this does not necessarily mean that they must be in hospital. Local circumstances vary, but in many cases, the family doctor, with the help of relatives on the spot, can provide all the necessary medication for pain control.

In Britain, it is primarily the responsibility of the family doctor to see that, at this time of great need, the families of the dying have all the benefits they are entitled to, but there is evidence that the community services are not used as much as they might be. Speaking at a symposium on the care of the dying at the Royal College of Physicians, Sheila Hancock said that when she was looking after her dying mother, she found a terrible lack of information about the facilities available to her. No one told her she was entitled to have district nurses, and she did not know about the Red Cross or the Marie Curie Foundation and the assistance they could supply.

It is hardly the fault of the local authorities that the facilities they provide are underused. In some cases, great efforts are made to inform the public but since no one can tell, in advance, who is going to require these services, the information often fails to get through. Your doctor will certainly see to it that you get your entitlement if you ask him.

Ideally, the doctor should act as a kind of coordinator of a team of helpers, and this team can be quite large. A good doctor interested in the care of the dying, will pay regular visits to see that all is going as it should, that pain control is complete, that the allocation of responsibility of care within the family is fair and reasonable and that the patient is encouraged to keep up interests in recreation and hobbies. The doctor should be as interested in the whole family as in the patient and should know all the members well. He should not be thought to be snooping if he enquires about the financial status of the family. He knows that when people are dying, there are often quite severe financial worries and that there are often ways of helping to relieve these – ways that he, or other members of the team, can tell you about.

After the doctor, the most important members is the district nurse. She should be involved at an early stage and she, too, will probably form a close relationship with the dying person and with the family. A good district nurse can be a tower of strength and will nearly always be able to solve the practical, day-to-day problems that inevitably arise. In most areas your doctor can ask for night nursing services, and in some areas, Macmillan nurses, who are specially selected, trained and skilled in this kind of work, may be available. If necessary, you may be able to get a grant, to help finance night nursing, from the National Society for Cancer Relief or from the Marie Curie Foundation.

Depending on requirements, the care team may also include a clergyman or priest; a social worker who can provide special skills in counselling and support; a specialist in pain relief; visiting experts from a hospice (see below); a physiotherapist; a chiropodist; and an occupational therapist. Don't forget the boost to morale that a visit from a hairdresser can provide. A simple explanation of the facts will usually be enough to prompt a local hairdresser to come along. Good reading vision may be of great importance to the dying and it is always possible to arrange for an optician to do an eye test at home.

Local authorities nearly always have transport services and these can be used for attendance at hospitals or dentists' surgeries if your own car is unsuitable. Recreational transport trips, with other people in a similar situation, are also commonly available and these outings are often greatly appreciated. Local voluntary organisations and charities are always ready to help in all sorts of practical ways. It should certainly go without saying that when questions of dental attention or new glasses arise, the worst thing you can do is to take the attitude that it isn't worth the trouble.

In Britain, the British Red Cross Society provides an excellent range of aids, such as walking sticks and other supports, wheelchairs, commodes, bedpans, urinals, and so on and they also run short courses for relatives looking after elderly and sick members of the family.

Here are some useful addresses:

National Society for Cancer Relief
Anchor House, 15-19 Britten Street,
London SW3 3TY

The Marie Curie Memorial Foundation,
28 Belgrave Square,
London SW1X 8QG

British Hospice Information Centre,
St. Christopher's Hospice,
51–55 Lawrie Park Road,
London SE26 6DZ

Macmillan Grants Department,
Michael Sobell House,
30 Dorset Square,
London NW1 6QL

British Association of Cancer United Patients (BACUP),
121–123 Charterhouse Street,
London EC1M 6AA

CancerLink,
46 Pentonville Road,
London N1 9HF

Compassionate Friends,
5 Lower Clifton Hill,
Clifton, Bristol

## Spiritual Help

The local church, too, will help, especially if the dying person has been a member. The benefit which the church can offer depends largely on the quality of the clergyman or pastor concerned. The approach of death, especially if appreciated by the patient, is a time of especial sensitivity to spiritual guidance, and religious observance, which may have been neglected for years, will often become important at this stage. Sometimes a deep preoccupation with religious questions is interpreted as 'mental confusion' and such a person will usually greatly welcome the presence of a person with whom these questions may be discussed in an open and unembarrassed way.

Ministers, priests and pastors have great demands on their time and often cannot undertake regular visiting throughout their growing parishes. But an appeal from a relative of a dying person will never go unanswered and it may be necessary to feel out, delicately, whether this is what the dying person would like. Church members, too, have become increasingly willing to engage in voluntary visitation. The Church of England has organised good neighbour schemes, called 'Fish Schemes' and these are widespread.

## The Hospice Movement

Next to loving care in a person's own home, a hospice for the incurably ill is best for those dying slowly from diseases such as cancer. The hospice movement has been one of the finest achievements of the medical profession. It was pioneered by people like Dame Cecily Saunders, who was a nurse and an almoner before becoming a highly qualified doctor and a person of great experience in the care of the dying. St. Christopher's Hospice, in Sydenham, London, founded in 1967, became a centre of research into these problems and a source of knowledge and inspiration to other doctors. In addition to the work done in St. Christopher's, the unit was able, from 1969 onwards, to extend hospice care to people in their own homes.

In 1974, a similar home-care service was set up in New Haven, Connecticut and this soon showed that excellent care for the dying could be afforded in their own homes in about three quarters of the cases. The same year, a unit called the Palliative Care Unit was opened in the Royal Victoria hospital, Montreal. This, like St Christopher's, was a full teaching and research unit, with home care teams. The following year, St Luke's Hospital, New York, set up a 'Symptom Control Team' to work alongside general medical staff in the wards and to help the community services organise a home care program.

Happily, the hospice movement is now spreading widely all over the world, carrying with it its message of hope and comfort for the dying. In Britain, hospices now care for about 40,000 families a year, controlling about 2,000 beds and with over 100 home-nursing support teams. In Britain and the USA there has been excellent support by the media and wide public approval, and many new hospices are being planned and built.

Hospice staff are the real professionals in the skills of caring for the dying, and their experience has shown that these skills must be based as much on compassion and understanding of the emotional needs of the patients as on expertise in the drug control of pain and death. The hospice is a place of trust and honesty where distress of mind, as well as of body, can be faced with directness and acceptance and can be relieved. Hospice doctors do not hesitate to use powerful drugs, when these are necessary, but they do pride themselves on the fact that they need these drugs less than others who do not have their experience in terminal care. Because of their understanding of priorities, these doctors and nurses commonly achieve full relief of distress without causing undue sedation or clouding of the minds of their patients.

## The Hospice Philosophy

Essentially, this is based on the principle that the existence of a serious illness, from which a person is unlikely to recover, does not deprive that person of hopes, needs, fears and rights. Such a person has exactly the same feelings and need for dignity as anyone else and has the same rights to be treated as a sensitive human being. There is a keen recognition that dying people suffer as much, or more, in the mind as they do in the body. Staff are well aware of how distressing may be the fear of death itself, regret over unfulfilled ambitions and unresolved conflict with others, worry about the future of others, worry over loss of the ability to look after others – all sorts of concerns.

So, after the skilled relief of physical pain, hospice staff are dedicated to the relief of mental pain. They do this by providing an environment in which patients are able gradually to see their way to talking about their emotional distress and freely expressing their hidden fears, confident that what they say will be treated with respect and kindness. Staff with long experience and detailed knowledge of the psychology of the dying, know how to answer difficult questions with directness and honesty, never forcing unwanted knowledge, but never being evasive or misleading when they know that the truth is wanted.

Another important element in the hospice philosophy is the recognition that proper management of the dying involves concern for, and the ability to cope with, the emotional problems of relatives. There is full recognition of the cardinal importance of the family for the well-being of the dying person and a sensitive awareness that unless the attitudes of the relatives to death and dying are right, the remaining time together will be marred for both the family and the patient. Again, openness and honesty are required and help towards a full understanding of the nature and purpose of grieving.

## Who Should Have Hospice Care?

There is no doubt that the ideal place to die is at home, surrounded, like Bill Bratwell, by caring relatives. But for many, this is impossible. Some have nursing needs which are beyond the capacity of the family; some have symptoms which the family find hard to take or even frightening; some need such constant attention that those available are simply no longer able to cope. Problems like incontinence, constant vomiting, bedsores, inability to eat, paralysis, and so on, may make it impracticable for the dying person to remain at home and you may feel you should explain this to your doctor and ask whether admission to a hospice is possible.

## A Peaceful Death

Experts in the care of the dying are agreed that, in the great majority of cases, the days, and sometimes even the weeks, prior to death are, or can readily be made, peaceful and free from struggle. Some deaths, of course, are so sudden and unexpected that nothing can be done to help. Such deaths, although particularly tragic for those left, need not necessarily demand our sympathy for the deceased – many die without any possible awareness of the fact and many others hope for such a death. By the majority reach a point of no recovery some time before death.

When this point is reached, the patient has to begin to learn to die. The dying person must be allowed, even, in the end, encouraged to die. Often, as we have seen, there is a tacit conspiracy on both sides to deny that the patient is dying, but, although understandable, this is usually wrong. Close friends, anticipating and fearing bereavement, may even force the dying person to pretend that he is not dying. These unhealthy attitudes deny the patient a great deal. They deny the chance to speak freely and to discuss the deep anxieties in the mind. They deny the dying person the dignity and support which are the rights of anyone in that condition. And they deny the chance to come to terms with the prospect of death and to have the benefit of all that is now known on the subject.

Learning to die is not a new thing. In the 15th century, at the very dawn of printing, William Caxton, working at the Westminster Press in 1491, published the *Art and Craft to Know ye Well to Dye*. This book, printed from wood-blocks in gothic type, was a best-seller and over 100 editions were made in the next 10 years. There is not much in Caxton's work that would help us today, but the commercial success of the undertaking testifies to the natural interest, at the time, in the subject. Regrettably, this interest has been replaced by a horror of the subject which has led us to repress all consideration of it, and we are all the losers.

A peaceful death comes to all of us, in the end. But the condition of your loved one during the weeks prior to that, depends very largely on your knowledge and attitude.

## Euthanasia

This question is a very real one, and not something to be dismissed with a shudder of horror.

We have seen that most members of the medical profession accept that when someone has reached the last stages of a fatal disease, there is no onus on them to try to prolong life by extraordinary means. Even when life might be extended a little by the continued use of life-support systems, or by intensive antibiotic treatment or blood transfusion, there comes a time, most will agree, when these measures can, and often should, properly be withheld.

But what of those who are mortally ill, in great pain of mind and body, and who wish to die, but whose illness is bringing life to an end with agonising slowness? There are many such people, dragging out a miserable existence with no hope of recovery, who long for 'easeful death' as a boon and a blessing. I need not list the kinds of distressing conditions that can bring about this stage. But there are many diseases so unpleasant that sufferers soon pass from the realisation that life is literally not worth living, to a state in which they desperately yearn for death.

Surveys have shown that many doctors have had requests to hasten death or end life. Very few have the courage openly to agree. The majority of doctors with responsibility for terminally ill patients do not, like Nicholas Parsons' Consultant, regard it as their primary responsibility to prolong life at all costs. Most feel that their first duty is to relieve suffering, and to do so by all necessary means, *even if these means might shorten life*. This is an important distinction.

Giving drugs which are effective in relieving pain but which involve the risk of depressing the respiratory centres in the brain and possible shortening life is quite different from deliberate killing. Stopping a treatment which was prolonging life but which was also adding to the miseries of the patient is also quite different from deliberate killing.

There is a good deal of support for the idea of euthanasia, but there are too many questions without clear answers. Who decides that the request of the dying person should be agreed to? Who decides whether the request is reasonable or made with sound mind? Might not circumstances change and result in a change of mind? At what stage in an incurable illness is it considered permissible to end life? How much suffering should be endured before the decision is made? How does one quantify suffering? How much influence should relatives or others have? What about demented old people who appear perfectly happy, but who are a burden to others? What about the mentally normal who know that they are a burden to others?

The truth is that it is impossible to apply logic to questions of this sort – and particularly when these questions are considered at the bedside of a person suffering an agonizing disease.

The making of difficult, often agonizing, decisions is part of medical professional duty. In spite of what has been said here about medical detachment, there are few if any doctors or nurses who can stand coldly by and watch their fellow creatures suffer.

# 5 The Psychology of Grief

Grief is a complicated and confusing state of mind. If you have recently suffered a bereavement, your mind will not be working too well, and your concentration is likely to be poor, so you may find some of this difficult to follow. But it is well worth making the effort for if you do, you will get at least some easement of your distress – possibly quite a lot.

A major feature of grief is a sense of helplessness and a tendency to go on hopelessly asking questions to which there is no ready answer. But that is not to say that there are no answers. Many of the important features of the grief reaction are now clearly understood. Obviously it is difficult for you, at this stage, to give much attention to anything other than your loss. The sooner you are able to concern yourself with other things, the better, but at this stage, the experience of grief is central to your consciousness. Perhaps a consideration of the very nature of what you are suffering may give your mind some acceptable alternative concern at this time when things are most difficult.

A very common feature of grief is a sense of guilt. For many, this may be one of the least bearable features of the experience. Much of the guilt experienced by the bereaved is neither reasonable nor justified and if you can understand how this guilt comes about, you may be able to obtain some comfort. There is almost always anger, and sometimes resentment, in grief. Many feel that this is wrong and allow it to add to their sense of guilt. When you understand how anger comes about, and realise how normal it is, you may be able to feel easier about this, too.

## THE PHYSICAL EFFECTS OF GRIEF

Grief is, of course, a mental state, but the relationship of the mind and the body is so close that the powerful mental effect of grief has a marked effect on the body. Different people are affected in different ways, and you may not have realised that some of the symptoms you are suffering are connected with your bereavement.

Early on, and sometimes over a long period, there are the waves of grief. The waves are highest at the beginning and closest together, but gradually get lower and further apart. When a wave hits you, the despair and distress reaches a peak of intensity. You have a sense of panic, a fluttering in your stomach, a tightness in your chest. You may feel your heart fluttering and you will probably give several deep sighs. These waves are due to release of adrenaline from the glands on top of your kidneys, and the glands are caused to do this by the intensity of your feelings. As you gradually adapt to the new life you have to face, these peaks of feeling will grow less intense and less frequent, and so will these unpleasant physical effects.

In addition to the waves, there is usually an on-going state which is also unpleasant. There is commonly a severe lack of appetite, and the majority of bereaved people lose quite a lot of weight. Many find that there is a persistent effect on the stomach, with a sense of fullness and even actual belching and heartburn. Sleeping is nearly always a problem, and as well as having difficulty in getting off to sleep, bereaved people often wake, early in the morning, to their unhappy thoughts. Some even wake during the night, to lie turning from side to side, their thoughts on an endless and pointless roundabout.

Irritability and jumpiness are extremely common. Bereaved people are always 'on edge' and are readily upset by trifles. They are forgetful, unreliable, inefficient – showing exactly the kind of behaviour you would expect from someone whose mind is intensely concentrated on something other than what they are doing. Headache, or, more commonly, a sense of pressure or tension in the head, is common, as are aches and pains all over the body.

You may wonder how these pains occur, and it is good that you should know, because understanding them may help to relieve them. I have mentioned the intimate relationship between the mind and the body and you will, by now, appreciate that not much can happen in the mind without some effect on the body. It is not only the muscles of expression in the face that reflect the state of the mind. Psychologists have long been aware that every part of the body commonly reacts to what is going on in the mind.

When you are tense, anxious, unhappy, stressed, your body reacts accordingly, mainly by the tight contraction of certain muscles. And if the mental state causing these contractions is a very prolonged one – as in bereavement – the muscle contraction will go on for an unnaturally long time and this leads to the accumulation of substances in the muscles which cause pain. These pain-causing waste materials are normally eliminated from the muscles at about the same rate as they are formed, but this is only possible if the muscles are allowed to relax and rest.

Unhappiness or distress of any kind commonly causes prolonged contraction in the muscles of the back of the neck and the scalp and this is by far the commonest cause of headache. About three quarters of all headaches – quite apart from bereavement – are caused in this way. Other muscles affected are those in the face, shoulders and back. Some people sustain contraction of the muscles which raise the jaw-bone in chewing and others tighten those around the eyes and in the forehead. Whichever muscles are affected, the result is pain in that region.

The cure is easier to understand than to apply. Relaxation sounds easy, but often requires the assistance of a skilled person such as a physiotherapist or a teacher of Hatha Yoga. But now that you know how these symptoms are caused, you may well be able to do quite a lot for yourself. One very interesting thing about all this is that the mind-body relationship is not a one-way process. Although the effect of the mind on the body is obvious, it is not so widely appreciated that the state of the body also has a marked effect on the state of the mind. Teachers of relaxation have long been aware that an unhappy state of mind which causes bodily tension, is itself relieved if the re-laxation is successful.

All these effects caused by the mind on the body – they are called 'somatic' effects, from the Greek word 'soma' meaning 'body' – have been known for many years but it can have a much more widespread influence than we had previously believe possible.

## Unexpected Bereavement

Several careful studies have been made of the reactions of those left behind, to the sudden and unexpected death of immediate relatives. These studies show that, especially with younger people, the sense of loss and the emotional disturbance are notably greater than when death was expected for some time. In one study of young widows, even as long as eight years after the death, those who had been bereaved with hardly any warning were more inclined to weep, to blame themselves, and to mourn than those who had had reasonable warning.

I don't want to suggest that this is always so. It is known, for instance, that with older people, the very close bond which often arises during a long illness, in which the sick person becomes wholly dependent on the other, may sometimes make the loss harder to bear than if such care had not been given.

## How Long Does It Last?

Mourning is an essential process. It is a process of recovery, as we shall see, and it is something that has to be gone through. It cannot be avoided. It takes time for new events to fill the terrible gap left by the departure of the loved one. These events are both mental and physical and they are the building bricks of your new life. So it is essential to *live* in order to overcome grief. You need contact with people and events, a chance to form new interests, to build a new life. Above all, you need time.

When I was an inexperienced doctor, working in the Army, I used to become so emotionally involved with the bereaved, especially with young soldiers' widows, that, knowing that time would reduce their distress, I would prescribe sedatives and tranquillizers to help them get through the time. I now know that this was a mistake. It is not the mere passage of time that matters. It is the conscious facing up to the facts, accepting them, the gradual coming to terms with the new situation and the building up of a new life, that slowly heals the wound. Putting people to sleep, and sedating them during the day, simply postpones the problem.

But the problem certainly exists and mourning is probably the worst experience of one's life. So naturally, we all want to know how long it is going to last. There is, in fact, no quick and precise answer to this question. The full intensity of the distress will usually be reached in about two weeks, and will then decline, sometimes very rapidly. With some people, the peak is delayed a little and with some the decline is slower. The easing of the full level of distress may take month. In most cases, about six months must pass before one can rely on any real freedom from recurring pangs of anguish. Many people need two years before they can feel entirely normal again.

These are average figures, probably reflecting a rough average of the degree of loss and the degree of dependence of the bereaved person. Some people are very self-sufficient, with relatively little dependence on others. The magnitude of the sense of loss will vary considerably.

Some people need to be told that the time for grieving is over – that they may, without guilt, begin to take a new interest in life and in other people. In the absence of someone to tell you when that time has come, you can use the advice in this book to enable you to decide for yourself.

## Loss

Few people recognise that grief and mourning are responses not only to the death of a loved one, but to any kind of loss. Strange as it may seem, the nature of grieving, the *symptoms* of grief are just the same whether the loss is that of a husband or wife or of the car which has been one's pride and joy. The strength of the grief is a measure of the size of the loss, whatever it may be, and for most people, the most valuable possessions they have are other people. The loss of another person need not even involve death. Separation and divorce, although obviously different from the death of a loved one, do involve something of bereavement, especially for the partner who did not wish it.

But loss of a person is not the only cause of bereavement. Many people value money, or even quite minor objects, more than they value people and there are numerous instances of people mourning loss of a fortune for years, sometimes never getting over it. When the New York stock market crashed in 1929, many ruined investors committed suicide. To these unfortunate people, money was clearly the most important thing in life and so the loss of it was the worst thing that could happen to them. The grief was more than they could bear and so they did away with themselves.

People grieve the loss of possessions. The response to burglary, for instance, is a form of mourning and produces all the symptoms of sudden bereavement. Not, perhaps, usually so strongly as after the loss of a person, but the effects, although less severe and less prolonged, are the same. The shock, the numbness, the inability to think of anything else, the memories – all are the same.

It is important to realise that the severity of the grief really does depend on the magnitude of the loss. Consider, for instance, a woman who had hated her husband for years – whose life had been made a misery by his selfish, demanding conduct, and who had, by him, been deprived of any sort of reasonable life. Do you think such a woman is going to mourn when such a husband dies? Certainly not. Obviously, she is likely to put on some brief show of a 'respectable' response to the death. Society assumes that bereavement is going to be distressing and expects mourning.

But it would be sheer hypocrisy to insist that, in such a case, tears, long faces, black clothes and separation from others were necessary or even appropriate. More commonly, the person lost is a person to whom the one left behind has become indifferent and with whom there has been little or no valued or useful interchange for years.Death in such a case may evoke some nostalgic memories of how things had been once upon a time, but the bereavement had already been over long before the death occurred. Such a bereavement was slow, a long succession of losses and pains, spread over years. And in many cases, the bereavement was actually inflicted by indifference or unkindness.

## Anger

Anger is a natural and normal response to an injury as severe as the loss of a loved one and you must not be either surprised or ashamed that you have experience it – and perhaps continue to do so. Anger is felt by the majority of bereaved people, often in short spurts of quite high intensity, with periods of depression in between, but sometimes as a slow, continuous smouldering bitterness. This causes you to become very irritable, touchy and difficult to be with, and you also probably have a feeling of insecurity or even danger.

There is more to anger than just a response to loss. If you can be truly honest with yourself, you may be able to admit that your anger has something to do with the less happy aspects of your former relationship. Few relationships are entirely perfect and many have a strong element of competitiveness, even fierce rivalry. These 'ambivalent' relationships often lead to a fantasy wish for the death of the other partner – a wish which remains acceptable so long as it *is* a fantasy. But the death of the partner arouses a powerful guilt response and this shows itself in anger.

One problem with anger is that it has to be directed somewhere. Often the anger is directed against self, but this may be found intolerable and the anger is directed elsewhere. The religious often direct their anger against God, for allowing, or even causing, such a thing to happen. This may lead to temporary, or even permanent, loss of faith. Anger is often wrongly directed. This can be unfortunate, and the short-term advantage can lead to trouble.

## Anger is Destructive

Anthea Croom-Dobson's husband Richard was a young and highly successful investment consultant. They had a generally happy and supportive, if sometimes stormy, relationship. There were two little girls, adored by their parents, and Anthea had given up an excellent job as an Assistant Principal in the Treasury, to look after them and help her husband with his promising career.

Richard had been employed by a long-established City firm of stockbrokers, but had, four years before, set up on his own to manage a series of new Investment Trusts. He had put a great deal of his own money into rent, staff salaries and advertising and was just beginning to see a return when he fell down while getting into his car and was found to have a fractured thigh bone. The break had occurred without any particular force and X-ray showed that the bone was abnormal at the site of the break.

Richard was admitted to hospital and fully investigated. The Consultant had asked Sister to tell him when Mrs Croom-Dobson visited, and he took her into his office and asked her to sit down.

'Your husband is finding it difficult to settle in hospital', he said, 'He's not a man who takes kindly to inactivity.'

'No, he never was. But this is a particularly difficult time – critical, in fact. His presence is essential if the whole business is not to crumble away. And the running costs are going on ...'

'Yes, I see. The trouble is –'

'Now that he is into a plaster, couldn't he get out? We can easily arrange a driver for him.'

'I'm afraid it's not as simple as that. The break was ... what we call a "pathological fracture"'.

'What's that?'

'The bone was almost eaten away. That's why it broke.'

'Good God! How did that happen?'

The Consultant was silent and after a moment she said, 'You don't mean it's ...'

'Yes, cancer. I'm most terribly sorry. I'm afraid it's very bad. We've done a full work-up. The primary cancer is in the prostate and there are secondaries in his lungs, liver and brain, as well as several bones.'

Anthea was quick to grasp the implications. 'Are you tell me,' she asked falteringly, 'that he is going to die?'

'I have to tell you the outlook is not very favourable. Of course we'll do a prostatectomy and try orchidectomy and stilboestrol, but I think you should prepare yourself ...'

Richard responded well, at first, to these treatments and some of the secondaries seemed to disappear. But he was never able to go back to work and, within less than a year, there was a massive recurrence and he died of haemorrhage in the lungs.

By then Anthea's affairs were in chaos and she was in a very bitter frame of mind. Richard's business had collapsed and he had made little insurance provision for the family.

Her closest friend tried to counsel her. 'You had a super job. I know you missed it. Why don't you –?'

Anthea flared up. 'Why don't you mind your own bloody business! You don't know anything about it!'

Others who saw this as the obvious solution to her problem were rewarded for their advice with the same sort of response, and it became clear that the subject of her work had a high emotional significance for her. None of them guessed that for years she had been harbouring resentment against her husband for the loss of her career.

So she sold the house in Camberley, to raise some capital and, hoping to keep in touch with some of their friends, moved into a tiny flat in the same area. She had suffered a great deal but, during the first few weeks after Richard's death, her chief emotion had been anger. This was directed chiefly against the family doctor who had been popular with both of them prior to Richard's death.

One day she visited the surgery.

'How are you, Anthea?'

She looked at him coldly. 'I haven't come to consult you about me,' she said, 'I want to know about the first two occasions Richard saw you about his prostate.'

The doctor looked at her warily. 'Of course,' he said, 'ask away.'

'I distinctly remember Richard telling me that you said he had a simply hypertrophy . . .'

'Well, yes, at the time, that's . . . how it seemed.'

'In other words, you missed the diagnosis.'

'You must understand – prostate cancer is quite uncommon in men of Richard's age –'

'You missed the diagnosis! Admit it. If you had been half competent, you would have spotted the cancer right away and a prostatectomy would have cured him.'

'Not necessarily . . .'

'Oh, come on! You know it. Did you do a rectal examination?'

'I see you've been reading the textbooks.'

'Did you?'

'Certainly. Each time I saw him.'

'And what did you find? Was the prostate much enlarged?'

'Moderately.'

'And hard? Was it hard and lumpy?'

'Look here,' said the doctor. 'What's the point of all this? Richard's dead. I'm desperately sorry. But I can't admit that I was in any way negligent.'

'We'll see about that.' said Anthea, and walked out of the consulting room.

Anthea went to see her solicitor who strongly advised her against legal action and she stormed angrily out of his office. At a citizen's advice bureau she was given the address of a lawyer who listened to her side of the case and, without much persuasion, agreed to help her to bring an action against the doctor.

He at once consulted his Medical Defence Union and their lawyers wrote an understanding but firm letter to Anthea, pointing out that, in their opinion, there were no grounds for the allegation of negligence and stating that if she persisted with the action, they would defend it.

'Well of course, they would say that, wouldn't they.' said her lawyer.

'I want to ruin that useless leech,' said Anthea, bitterly, 'just the way he ruined me. Let him feel what it's like.'

In his summing-up, the judge expressed sympathy with her in her loss, showed understanding with her feelings, expressed clear disapproval of those who had encouraged her to litigation, and made it plain that he thought her action had no substance in law. The finding went against her and she became responsible for heavy costs, as well as for her own lawyer's and counsel's fees.

Anger can be helpful, for a time, but, in the long term, it is a destructive emotion and must be resolved. Sustained anger drives people away. It can become self-indulgent and very unattractive and those who engage in it become isolated and lonely. So try to understand the causes of your anger. Face up to them. Understand them. Then put them aside and start living positively again.

### Guilt in Mourning

It is easy to confuse the different parts of the response to the death of someone who is close. Many people, who had drifted apart, are going to suffer a sense of guilt because of a suspicion that they may have been, at least partly, responsible for the gradual separation. But such guilt, although unpleasant, is not the same as mourning, which is a response to loss. So let us take a look at the question of guilt.

Guilt is a feature of mourning, even in those cases where the quality of the relationship has been high and the mourner has seemed to have done everything possible for the deceased. This apparently strange fact is easily explained. Death is such a major event that it is impossible to be logical about it. To have such a terrible thing happen to someone close, against all reason and justice, severely shakes our faith in the orderliness of events, and we tend to revert to a more primitive or superstitious frame of mind.

'What can have caused this?' a widow might ask herself, 'Could it have been because I encouraged him to work too hard? He knew how much I wanted that coat, so he just pushed himself that little bit too far. It's entirely my fault that he died.'

Thoughts of that kind are very common and lead to guilt. Often, the mental processes leading to guilt are remarkably irrational. One woman sustained guilt for months because her husband had, once or twice, expressed the desire for black puddings, a desire she had never got around to gratifying.

When death ends unhappy relationships, guilt can occur for another reason. This has to do with society's expectations of how a bereaved person should feel. Because bereavement is normally shattering, a failure to show the predictable response is thought to be almost indecent, and when the person left behind does not feel these expected emotions, he or she may feel guilty.

If you are in such a case, I hope you will soon be able to get enough detachment to see the matter as it really is and to accept that there is no onus on you, whatsoever, to act the hypocrite and to pretend to grief you do not feel. It is perfectly natural and proper to have a sense of relief at the ending of a painful and damaging relationship. There is a world of difference between wishing to be separated from someone who is damaging your life and wishing that person to be dead. Of course, as we have seen, there may have been such a wish – probably barely expressed, or perhaps guiltily acknowledged and hastily dismissed from the mind. This is a common feature of ambivalent relationships, as Freud pointed out.

But if any such thoughts have occurred, the subsequent death of the person thought about is bound to lead to a strong sense of guilt. The guilt may be released in anger, but often it is not.

'I wished he was dead, and now he is. So I've caused his death.'

This is a common pattern, seldom admitted to, but often in the minds of the widowed, and it is hard to comfort such people. Talking about it can certainly help. Trying to remember exactly how it was, without exaggerating. Bearing in mind that the wish was only intermittent and occurred at times of particular exasperation. Wishing someone dead is seldom really serious – most of us try, from time to time, to see things from the point of view of the other person, and one need only do this to appreciate the full horror of a genuine wish for someone else's death – the sort of wish that might be reflected in action. It is barely thinkable.

Discussing the matter with others helps to get it into perspective and one usually sees that such a wish was just a sort of fantasy, such as a child might have. The stroke club movement, which is now flourishing in most countries has been of immense help to the relatives and carers of stroke victims, who meet each other and discuss their common problems. One of the unexpected things that has come out of these conversations between carers has been the frequency with which guilt arises from thoughts of this sort. Many have found great relief in expressing these thoughts and in finding that others have them, too.

**Hallucinations of the Bereaved**
I have decided to include a short reference to this apparently strange matter for a good reason. Hallucinations certainly occur. The study of the experience of a large number of bereaved people has shown that almost half of them have had, and often continue to have, some kind of hallucinatory experience of the dead person – feeling their presence, hearing their voices, even catching grief glimpses of them. They may, often in a particularly real and convincing way, feel that the loved one is upstairs, making the familiar noises, perhaps whistling a well-known tune, calling out one's name.

But those who have these experiences are unlikely to talk about them, even to close friends, and this suggests that there may be some fear that they are abnormal and possibly even an indication of mental instability. If you have had, or continue to have, hallucinations of this kind, you should know that they are accepted by the experts as being entirely normal, and indeed helpful, features of the bereaved state.

These hallucinations often last for many years, but are commonest in the first ten years. They are most likely in older people, after a long marriage and especially if the marriage has been a happy one, and if there have been children. The most frequent – experienced by about 40 per cent – is a strong sense of the presence of the dead person. About 14 per cent have a hallucination of seeing the deceased and about the same proportion hear the deceased's voice. About 10 per cent actually find themselves talking normally to the deceased and a very small number – about 3 per cent – feel themselves touched by the dead person.

Bereavement hallucinations are the result of unconscious wishes for the presence of the deceased, wishes that lead either to the misinterpretation of other sensations, or even to the stimulation of the perceptive parts of the brain so as to produce the effects wished for. The illusion of the presence of the dead person is often comforting, and some bereaved people welcome this and deliberately try to foster it. Most who have it, find it helpful.

The hallucinations of bereavement only rarely cause distress and should, on the whole, be welcomed.

**Unusually Severe or Prolonged Mourning**
You may quite probably feel that the degree of distress and anguish you are suffering is much worse than average, and you may be right. The degree of suffering *does* vary considerably, depending on a number of factors.

The loss of a son or daughter, for instance, is often a graver blow than the loss of a close adult, and this is especially so if, as so often happens, you had begun to live through the young person, talking compensation, perhaps, for your own disappointments in life by observing the successes of the one who has died. This is a truly tragic situation, and is often harder to bear than the loss of a very young child. In such a case, mourning is likely to be very prolonged and severe, and the rebuilding of your life is likely to seem a greater task than you think you can cope with. Living through others is not always the best or safest way of life, and this is one of the reasons. As we shall see, the conquest of bereavement, is a process of rebuilding a new life in the absence of the loved one, and if the rest of your life is not to be ruined, this is what, somehow or other, you have to do.

Sudden death is always harder to take than a death which has been anticipated for a long time, and mourning after sudden death is usually more severe and prolonged. Experience shows that when death is expected, the mourning process begins before death and may have been going on for quite some time before the loss becomes absolute. This is not to say that the distress at the time of death may not be severe, but that the duration and intensity of mourning, after death, is usually less. These are broad generalisations and so many factors apply that every case is different.

A bereavement as a result of suicide must be one of the hardest of all things to bear. For to all the other causes of distress is added the conviction that the death is somehow our fault – that we have failed to provide sufficient love or attention to make life worth living for the dead person, or failed to perceive the terrible suffering which drove the suicide to that dreadful extremity. Such a situation is very difficult to live with and if this has happened to you, you are going to need all the detachment you can muster to be able to see the facts as they really are.

A great many suicides are accidental and were not really intended. Many of them are 'suicide gestures' – cries for help – which went tragically wrong. I hope that, on consideration, this may be some consolation. The cry for help reached you, all right, but, as things worked out, you were in no position to respond to it. Had you known how serious matters were, you undoubtedly would have taken helpful action. Many suicide attempts are made for quite flimsy reasons and may merely indicate the desire for more attention. Certainly, such attempts seldom succeed, but any form of attempted suicide is a dangerous business, and sometimes they do.

The next thing to remember is that the majority of genuine suicides actually do indicate that there was some, perhaps temporary, mental illness at the time. The causes of such mental disturbances are not well understood – most of them are a form of schizophrenia – but one thing is certain, and that is that the disturbance is not the fault of those left behind. You cannot, in reason, accept all the blame if the balance of the mind was disturbed.

**Respect for the Dead**
'De mortuis, nil nisi bonum' 'Of the dead (speak) nothing but good.' This has been the principle in the past, originating, perhaps in a super- stitious fear that the spirits of the dead were around us and might do us harm if we were not sufficiently respectful. Whatever the reason, it is clear that a great deal of hypocrisy and nonsense has resulted. Recently, I took a walk through a wonderful old overgrown cemetery and could not help wondering at the motives behind the many large and elaborate tombstones and mausoleums, most of them overgrown with foliage and leaning at all angles, which fill the place. These expensive and elaborate relics almost all bore statements eulogising the dead, and one thing is certain – very few of these statements were true.

Of course we remember the best aspects of the departed, and there is no harm in a little exaggeration, but it is healthy and honest also to remember the bad. And if, as a result, we mourn a little less deeply, there is no harm in that either.

Bereavement is bad enough without adding to your distress by having guilt feelings about not mourning enough. The intensity of your grief is a measure of the seriousness of your loss, not a measure of the virtue of the one who has died. Your loss has to do with many things beside that. The one who has died has not suddenly become a saint.

It may be that an element in your grief – perhaps a large element – is a strong feeling of distress on behalf of the person who has died. This seems to be a common reaction, but it is unreasonable. The matter was well put by Socrates, at his trial, two and a half thousand years ago:

'There are two alternatives – either death is a state of nothingness and complete unconsciousness, or the soul passes from this world to another. Now, if you suppose that death is like the sleep of one undisturbed even by dreams ... then to die is gain, for eternity is but a single night. But if death is the journey to another place, and there, as men say, all the dead abide, what good, my friends and judges, can be better than this?'

Socrates is acknowledged as being one of the two or three wisest men who ever lived and he has had a greater influence for good on western civilisation than anyone other than Jesus Christ, so I think we might take his word for it on this point and accept that there is no call to pity the dead.

# 6 The Experience of Bereavement

Grief is a reaction to loss, usually, but not necessarily, of a person. This is the account, given by a sensitive, intelligent woman, of the death of her much-loved dog.

**Death of Admiral**

'We knew for some years that Admiral had to die. He had been ill for a long time. Often he would moan all night, in pain. It was as if he were doing it to annoy us. I used to go down to try to stop him. Once or twice, when we were very tired from lack of sleep, looking after him, I hit him with a rolled paper to quiet him. I'm very guilty about that. I still wake up dreaming about it – because he really was in pain.'

'The morning before he died I knew it was the end, because when I phoned the vet he said, 'Bring him in. It's serious'. But I didn't want to take him, because I knew he would be put down. I went to my class. I was very slow. In the end I took Admiral to the vet. Peter met me there. He was very sweet. I felt fear, sweating, palpitations, numbness. There was a strong need for social obligation, like thanking the vet, very formally. I had dreaded this occasion for so many years, but Admiral was a great drain on us and sometimes I almost hoped he would die. He was in great pain.'

'The vet said, "Let's be brave and do it now." He went out and left us alone with Admiral for a while. Peter was very nice. After the injection he looked Admiral in the eyes. He thought it would be a comfort for Admiral to feel someone with him as he died. I remember at the point of death the eyes went opaque. There wasn't much physical difference. The vet left us with the dog. I actually laughed. I think the others understood that it was hysteria. I was responding slowly. It was as though I had a tape recorder in my head that recorded at the time, but I had to play it back later to understand what had happened.'

'I didn't cry. I nearly cried but it was as though we had both decided not to cry. We let the vet arrange the cremation. I felt like a cheat. My sister, who worked for a vet said, "No matter what they say, they always send the bodies to a glue factory." The vet said this was nonsense. For the first few days I didn't feel emotion. I felt I ought to but it came out later.'

'I don't miss looking after him, but I miss the routines like going for walks. I still grieve for him. At first we were very busy getting rid of his stuff. I dumped his bed. I didn't cry then. I think I displaced my grief. I would get very upset about other things, like deaths in the paper.'

'I actually did love Admiral, but he wasn't a human being. I shall continue to wake up in the night feeling guilty. The guilt is still there. It has replaced my anxiety dreams about his getting lost, when he was a puppy.'

## Reactions

Each person's experience of grief is unique, and each one has something to teach us. Here is the account of an Austrian woman, one of many people interviewed for this book.

'I was making dinner when his boss knocked on the door. He looked uncomfortable. He was itchy. I said, 'What's the matter?'

'He said, "Bad news. Richard died in a motor accident." Richard was in Hong Kong.

'My first thought was, "Oh my God! How am I going to tell the children? How do I tell the kids?"

'They were upstairs. While we talked, I already tried to work out how to tell each of them and how to have physical contact with each of the three. I was very upset. A neighbour was brought in. I didn't know her very well. I didn't want the children to get wind of it. I wanted to protect them. I thought, "Why has *she* come in? She doesn't usually come in. It's an intrusion."

'After they had left, my oldest son (14) came down. I told him. He was very upset and said, "I want to go for a walk."'

'I said, "You go, but don't be too long." And then I told the other two.'

'When my son was out, the good woman across the road got hold of him, took him in the house and said, "Now you're the oldest one, you have to be brave, you have to support your mother." How can you do something like *that* to a child! I found that so terrible – that people want to take over, and to intrude, and they don't leave you to cope, or stand back and wait to see how you cope, and then . . .'

'Maybe I had a bad experience, but I found *that* the most awful thing, more even, . . . well really terrible! I also resented her being there at first. I tried to get her out and said I was perfectly all right and would call her if I needed her. She wanted to tell the children and that was *absolutely not on!* I was adamant. I don't think she had experienced bereavement herself.'

'Charley cried a lot. Karen didn't cry at all, which worried me afterwards, quite a bit. She only said, "Oh, my daddy!" I wasn't going to cry – typical of me – not in front of the kids. So I did all my crying at night. Having to think about the kids was a help. I concentrated on them and all my thoughts were to keep as calm as possible, for their sake.'

'The grief came later. I was so involved with coping, that the grief didn't hit me until night. During the day there were so many demands that nine times out of ten the grieving came at night when the kids were in bed. It was a bit unusual because I didn't see the body. He died in Hong Kong in this car accident – they couldn't bring him back ... the heat. There was just the funeral service when they buried the ashes. In a normal death you see the body. He travelled a lot – he was often away. The worst thing to cope with was the weekends when he would have been at home. Weekends were awful. During the week I could kid myself and say, "Oh, he's abroad and he's coming back." That way it all, well, progressed.'

'There was a stage when I wasn't quite sure how he died. There were four people in the car and one came out alive. There was a fire. So I was always asking myself, was he dead, was he unconscious immediately, or was it a horrid death? But I never voiced that. He was only 40. We had been married 17 years.'

'I haven't got over it – I don't think you ever get over it. I have adjusted to it. There were various stages. There was a stage when I thought, "I don't want to go on. I am fed up. I have the responsibility for the kids and everything, and he got it light." And then the stage where I thought, "He doesn't grow old. He had the easy way out." Another stage – it's difficult always to go places on your own. You can make the children your life, but that's not fair on them. And now they are at the stage where they want to do things on their own, so you have to completely re-establish yourself.'

'Charley, the middle one, still cries an awful lot – even after six years. That's how he copes with his grief. The little one didn't cry and I was quite worried because she was daddy's darling ... I bought her a pony. She dearly loves the pony. If anything ever happened to the pony ... Geoffrey missed him very much because they had this ritual – they got up in the morning and they went running together, then in the bathroom Richard shaved and Geoffrey showered and they had conversations and discussions. He missed that very much. I tried to go running with him, but I'm not much good at running up the hill at six o'clock in the morning, even six years ago.'

'They are all now fairly balanced and recovered. I can't say how long it took.'

'Sleep was a big problem. I cried at night ... cried myself to sleep. Not sleeping went on for a long time – a year or even more – also – don't laugh – if I just had one of the kids in bed with me I slept better. I don't know if it was the body contact or what. Maybe you're more alert if you are on your own. It was bad by three o'clock – I could have screamed. In bed by twelve, still awake at three. I tried to read but my eyes had deteriorated and I couldn't focus. This happened quite suddenly. I had to get reading glasses. I didn't take pills.'

'My father-in-law's sister is still on pills after five years. Mind you, she's older. She lost her mother and then, two years after, her husband. Her mother was 84. It was expected. But she had a hard time because she kept blaming herself – quite unnecessarily – for things she had, or should have, done. There was no way she was to blame. She went to therapy lessons. She's still not got over it.'

'I spent a lot of time with this separated woman. She said, "I wish I were in your position." I said, "Look, for you the husband is still there for the children to ask Dad for help. Mine can't."

'I found it difficult having no adult conversation. I had friends, but with your husband it's different. The relationship is different. Over the years you grow together and then, all of a sudden, that's gone. In the evenings, when the kids have gone to bed, I am alone with TV for a long time. For about a year, I went to a neighbour across the road every night at about ten o'clock. We would chat about the news or something, and then I would go home to bed. That helped me a lot – to see some adults at the end of the day.'

'I found out a lot about myself being on my own. An awful lot of people offer help, but never anything concrete. You are so involved with yourself, you can't think what to ask for. If someone had said, "Shall I bake a cake, or cut the grass?" I would have said, "Oh, yes!" If they had only offered to take the children out or cook a meal, or something definite like that, I could have said, "Yes" or "No". It was too difficult to think, out of the blue, what they could do for me. So I did it myself. There's so much to do.'

'I didn't blame myself over Richard's death. My philosophy is that each one of us has a clock that is set when we are born and whatever you do you can't avoid it. His clock was set. One thing that helped me was that we tried to make the most of the life we had, tried to make the most out of every opportunity. You can always wish you had done this or that, and I don't say he had done everything he wanted to, but he did all he could. It also helped me, later, to think that he had got the better deal – not getting old.'

'It is terribly important to keep very busy. Not to blame. Talk about it if you feel you want to. I kept on talking about Richard did this or that, and, without realising, putting it in the present, not in the past. Don't fight against it, but keep busy. Don't fight insomnia – take up a hobby – use the hours. This morning I woke up at 4.30 and I'm still here this evening. You don't die of lack of sleep. You can always make up later – have a nap in the afternoon.'

'Responsibilities kept me going. I had to carry on for the kids. That helped. I can't say how I would have been on my own. I would, perhaps, have gone over the top and just travelled the world, or something like that. I sometimes ... well I feel that the kids miss out a bit. But I've done all I can. That's all ...'

## Loss of a Best Friend

The severity of grief depends on the size of the loss and this, in turn depends on how much the person we have lost mattered to us. Grief is the price we pay for loving, or for caring, or even simply for depending on someone else. Here is how one man – a quiet, undemonstrative and successful graphic designer, described the loss of a friend.

'I had known for four or five years that Magnus had a lung problem and that it could get serious at any time. He had been on a plane to America and because of his breathing it had had to be diverted to Newfoundland. On and off, I had been quite close to him – we'd been together at Art School. He was slightly older than me, he was more mature and I looked up to him and sought his advice. He was a sort of mentor. We met for lunch and I saw him quite often.'

'I remember one day realising he was having breathing trouble. He was a person who demanded a lot of himself and had very high standards. He was a marvellous craftsman – someone I wanted to emulate. I was always pleased if he approved of something I'd done. When this breathing problem got severe he had to reduce his work. It was very shocking to me when he gave up work, because he had always been a man who did so much. He had always put more into a job than was asked, and would never take the easy way out.'

'His chest got so bad that he couldn't risk catching a cold. Once we had to leave in the middle of dinner because I was developing a cold. When we saw how his wife reacted, I realised for the first time how serious it was. Later he caught a cold from someone else at a party and that brought on his final illness. I would have felt terrible if it had been me.'

'Magnus became more mellow, in a way, and nicer, when he was ill. He had been an abrasive character before, and highly critical. He had this idea of making the most of the time he had left – of enjoying everything to the full. At one point he asked my wife to recommend a counsellor because he didn't know how to cope with the situation – but he obviously did. He was quite happy in the final years because he just decided to do the things he wanted to. He had a pension or something and stopped doing commercial work. He was always keen on craftsmanship, learning techniques, and so on.'

'But I think it got quite difficult for his family because they had to run and fetch things all the time. He probably vented his feelings on them, a bit. He was slightly irritating because he was always so good at everything. He would suddenly take up gardening and produce the most marvellous garden – having never done it before.

'When his daughter phoned, I was shocked. I knew what she was going to say. She told me that his final illness had been quite short and that he had died. That was about three years ago. It was a while before I reacted fully. Then I felt that the world I related to had been distorted – because he had been a point of reference, you know. It was as though one of the planets had disappeared and all the others had to move to compensate. It's a bit like when an elderly relative dies – say a grand-parent – and you realise that there are fewer and fewer people to look up to and you are more on your own. Soon you will be the oldest person. No one to look to for help and advice.'

'Even after his death, if I did anything I was pleased with – like a drawing or decorating the house – I would think, "I wonder what Magnus will make of this ..." Now it's up to me to do things on my own and not to ... emulate people – that's the feeling.'

'I was surprised at the number of people at the funeral – sixty or seventy. There were some quite distinguished designers and so on who esteemed him. His father was there. He had a lot of friends and that was an emotional occasion. I felt influenced by the others. I felt like crying.'

'It became almost a party at the end. We had a great feeling that we ought to do something to commemorate him – like a memorial or something. We tried to get some of his friends interested and they did want to do something, but it faded out and we haven't done anything yet. I feel responsible to his wife and children if they need help. I don't think they do. We see them still.'

'I do still grieve. Magnus had been important in my life since I was seventeen. I like to visit his house. It's still very much as it was with so many things he made in it. It is very much *his* house. In a way, the house is a memorial to him. He was a craftsman – he made his own memorial.'

## A Long Time A-Dying

Many feel deeply guilty at the recollection of their wish for the death of a partner. But when the terminal illness is prolonged and the suffering of both, and the strain on the carer, just go on and on, such a wish may be natural and normal.

'You wouldn't believe what can happen when a once-loved partner takes a long time to die. The demand on the emotions is terrible. In the end they just get used up. It's horrible. You get to hating him – and, at last, there is nothing left but your obsession with how long it is taking. It's so abnormal, you wonder if you are going mad – if you are some kind of monster. But you know you are not. You're just so tired. So terribly tired.

'How do I feel now? Alone ... Very alone. Guilty sometimes. I get these primitive ideas of retribution. But mostly just angry – so angry, sometimes, that I can think of nothing else.'

**Getting Help**

'I did not want sympathy. Here in Spain, it is the custom for neighbours and friends, indeed even passing acquaintances to call, express their condolences and administer a sympathetic kiss. I couldn't bear it. After a while I locked the door and hid in the bedroom.

'When a dear friend came to me and offered practical help in a matter-of-fact voice, I knew that this was all I could take. A friendly hand and help with those things which had to be done, but which were impossible or incredibly difficult to do. A message to be delivered, letters to be written, a car and a willing driver made available. Yes these, but no more.

'Later, when I had to talk, I was glad indeed to find a quiet listener. I didn't want to be consoled. I wanted time to sort things out for myself; to face my fears and my desolation. I was, at that time, totally numb and incapable of generating enough energy to take any action without encouragement and help.

'The thing is – suddenly you are no longer a whole person. You are only part of a person. You continually look for the part of you that is there no longer. You don't want to do anything, yet you must fill your emptiness with *something.*

'All those friends who gathered round immediately after he died, said, "We'll keep in touch". For many, those were the last words they said to me. They just drifted away.

'I don't want to lean. I have learned to be by myself and listen to my music – but I do terribly miss companionship.'

Another lady described her loss graphically and she, too, emphasised the need for practical help.

'They say that in war, when a man is shot, he doesn't feel any pain at first – just a numbing blow. That's what happened to me. His death was totally unexpected. He was killed by a runaway truck. When I was told, I felt nothing. Nothing at all. There was just a blank numbness. I didn't speak. I didn't cry. I put down the telephone and went on dusting the room, and then I sat down and looked at the wall. This couldn't be true. It couldn't be happening. I must do ordinary things then life would continue as before.'

'It was only after three days that the pain came. Then I was glad to see my friends and was grateful for their help. The worst was when they came in and broke down as they sympathised; the best was when they saw without being asked what help was needed in ordinary things that *had* to be done. I wasn't capable of thinking of these things without help.'

**Who is Going to Mend It?**
'There were things in the home that he always did. Like buying the wine, filling in the forms, investigating a column of ants in the bedroom, unblocking a sink – I simply don't know how to begin . . . Look, my cigarette lighter won't work – who is going to mend it?'

## Loss of a Mother
This is a further extract from the account, started in Chapter 4. The speaker is intelligent, introspective, and angry. Her statement brings out many important points.

'For a long time – even before my mother died – I cried myself to sleep every night and had nightmares. It was worse after her death. I had sort of known for years that she was going to die. You think you are prepared but you are not – being intellectually prepared is not the same as being emotionally prepared – any more than you can be prepared for the view from Everest or your first orgasm. These things are so powerful that however much you know about them, or have read about them, they take you absolutely by storm, and so it was with this. I was amazed at how unprepared I was. Beforehand, you feel that you're clever, that you've foreseen what is going to happen, but when it *actually* happens it's as though you never expected it at all. So devastating – so different – not like any book.

'I suppose I was all right for four or five days, just going on in a state of numbness, being very practical. My sister was just the same – we were quite efficient. But I had an awful feeling just of a hole in the middle with something missing. Awful anguish. I hated every little old lady just for being alive – I felt they had no right to be alive.

'I had dreadful nightmares about coming back and finding the whole place empty. This was because my father had cleared *everything* out when we went down the day of the funeral. He insisted on going through things and that was awful. The nightmares were different every night and that went on for about six weeks and then off and on for about two years. They are less frequent now after two and a half years.

'Friends were all right to talk to, but really they are embarrassed by death. They don't want to talk about death. Some people just giggled – didn't even say "I'm sorry." It's very irritating – perverse – when people laugh at such things. One friend was terrific. She's a free-lance journalist working very hard. She listened and she understood. She knows about psychology and about people and about death. She understood what I was feeling and that what I was feeling was normal. That was a tremendous help.

'After the devastation, the thing I felt was *anger*. Particularly when my sister started telling me all the things I didn't know that my mother had told her. She had to unburden herself. We are very close and were both close to our mother. She's a lovely girl – very different from me … She told me about the things he did – not only the financial things, little bits of chicanery, the humiliations.

'My sister had preserved the illusion of his virtue for so long – as though he were in some way removed from ordinary people and more moral and better. And then to realise that he was actually a good deal less moral than most people was a great shock.'

'I absolutely adored my pa, when I was small. It wasn't until I was about thirteen that I began to realise that he was an absolute charlatan. When you are small you accept everything your parents do. He was a poseur, lecturing on Moral Philosophy with his golden voice. Adored by his students. He was totally insincere and, in everything he did, a hypocrite. There's nothing personal in this – I just started seeing these things in a totally objective way.

'The way he treated Mamma and rode roughshod over her! He sent me to boarding school and I actually stopped going home for the holidays because it was so painful. These blazing rows . . . He resented me so much. Later at University, I never went home at all. My sister could get round him – she's this little blonde thing and could make him laugh – she could manage him. She feels much the same as I do about him, but on the surface she was closer.

'My mother never told me how unhappy she was – I would have been able to help her more if I had known. I thought she really was quite fond of him and wanted to be repressed and submissive. I suppose I despised her slightly for having given in and it was only in the very last month that I realised what a struggle her spirit was having all the time. She had brought us up to be loyal to someone who didn't deserve that loyalty, and the cost was the damage to my own warm relationship with her. Every time I tried to get close to her she got worried that he would feel I was taking her away from him and slightly pushed me away after a bit. Then she got guilty about that. She just believed that marriage was a sacrament, a commitment, and that she'd made her choice and must be loyal no matter what he did.

'Realising the depth and duration of her unhappiness left me an awful legacy of wretchedness and bitterness . . . to realise that the mother we had loved had just died and to discover that her whole life had been wasted on someone who wasn't worth it and that she had had very little happiness . . . You feel all these "if only" things which are so destructive. If only I had known, I would have got her away somehow and given her some happiness. She had a great capacity for enjoyment and she could have come to London.

'I started getting infections, about every six weeks, and I didn't know why. I now know that after a bereavement the immune system is compromised. I went to my doctor who more or less said, "Don't waste my time." I told him that my mother had just died and that I had had three doses of 'flu – very bad – gastric and ear, nose and throat viruses – one after the other. That normally I was very healthy and just don't get things. He was hopeless. It was only through reading a book that I realised . . . My journalist friend said that physical illness is one of the responses to bereavement – your immune system is in a very low state. You are producing adrenaline.

'Physical activity does help. Exercise suppresses the production of adrenaline and encourages the production of lymphocytes. A professional should know about that – they set themselves up as God and then they let you down. If someone had just said, "Look, this is a natural part of grieving – that you get these things." There should be a pamphlet or something available. My nails and hair were in a bad way and I was spotty. I was more accident-prone as well. I could be efficient at pure mechanical drudgery and I liked doing things I normally hated – like ironing. I just couldn't cope with writing letters about complex subjects like prisoners of conscience – I just wanted to scrub the sink. I would bump into things, forget things, drop things. My driving was safe because my reactions were slower.'

'Two years after she died, I went to this wonderful place in India where I did nothing but climb rocks and swim. One morning I woke up with this amazing feeling – as though my brain was flooded with light – and the sentence in my mind was,

"All that matters is that she died knowing you love her."

I had an amazing feeling of liberation as though a great burden had dropped from me. That was incredible. It took all that time.'

# 7 How to Cope with Grief

## GRIEF MUST BE EXPRESSED

Anthropological research has shown how, in many societies, people react to death in a formal, ritualistic way and perform ceremonies which involve the active participation of the whole family and even the whole tribe.

To these people, death is an important and accepted major event, giving status to the bereaved. The ceremonies are open, public and often prolonged. They encourage free and loud expression of grief. In contrast, our modern rationalistic culture has left us with no proper substitute for the earlier process. But, for all our sophistication, we are still basically the same kind of people – especially in our emotions.

The modern 'stiff upper lip' concept which preaches restraint, the avoidance of any show of emotion, and a contempt for those who howl in the market-place, has actually made it much harder for the bereaved. People like you are now expected to suffer in silence, to show an impassive face, and not to embarrass others with your grief.

It's a pity our present cultural patterns do not allow you to run out into the street, tear your clothing, and scream out your sorrow and pain – no doubt you would like to. Pain and grief cause bodily tensions, which when prolonged, are in themselves, painful. Crying can release these tensions.

More important than this, however, is for you to understand the true nature of the process of recovery from mourning. It is not a matter of just 'getting over it'. When people say that time will heal the hurt they are saying something that is untrue. It is not the passage of time that makes things easier. If you were put to sleep by a doctor the day after your bereavement, kept unconscious for a year, and then allowed to recover, you would feel the same intensity of grief you were experiencing when you went to sleep. Time, in itself, has nothing to do with it. It is what happens to you during the passage of time that causes the difference.

All life involves change. Throughout life we are constantly exposed to new experiences of all kinds; we store away data in our memories, and with each additional item of information, we change. Ideally, change should involve growth – growth of the mind and the personality, growth of wisdom. When we have shared life intimately with another person, this growth is a dual process and the other person becomes part of us. This is the main reason why bereavement is so painful. But it is also the reason why, after bereavement, we cannot live exclusively on the past. As we shall see, it is right and valuable to cherish and preserve every possible memory of the person we have lost, for, at the time of the bereavement, we are still very dependent on that person. We need to remember and we should do all we can to retain as much as possible. We should take every opportunity to talk about the deceased.

But to deny the normal processes of further life development is deadly. You have no choice but to accept that the processes of change will go on and that you will now change in a different way from the way you would have gone had you not been bereaved. The way will be different but not necessarily worse. You are going to have experiences which will modify your mind and personality and these experiences will not be shared, or commented on, by the loved one who has died. So you are going to become a different person from the person you would have become. You may not like this, but there is nothing you can do about it.

Bereaved people often speak of being 'cut in half' or of losing half of themselves and this is a very real experience. But the missing half has to be replaced, or filled up, and this requires new living, new input. Some have the resources to do this on their own. Others find that an 'aching void' persists until they find someone new to help to fill it. Clearly, for some, the solitary state is unnatural, and, however unfeeling it may seem to replace the beloved with another, this is often the right thing, eventually, to do. The need is often recognised by one partner while the couple are still together and it is not uncommon for a husband or wife to make it plain to the other that remarriage would be approved of, after bereavement.

## How to Take the Funeral

Although different people react to the funeral in different ways, near-ly everyone recognises that it is an important event. Like christening and marriage, a funeral is a 'rite of passage' and these rites all have a psychological and social function. You may still be at the stage of shock so that the funeral releases no emotions in you, or you may be so broken that you are sure you could not bear to go through with it. Even so, the funeral is important. It is a formal, public, taking leave – a saying 'goodbye' to your loved one – a relinquishment, even, sometimes, however good the partnership, a freeing from old bonds and a licence to proceed to a new life.

In most cases, friends and relatives genuinely do feel for the bereaved and the funeral is an occasion when that feeling may be freely expressed. This is often very comforting. Although it is now often considered right to repress the expression of grief, and for many, calm impassivity at the funeral seems proper, this is a mistake. The funeral is one occasion on which even contemporary social attitudes allow you to show your distress.

We need ritual, and there is little enough of it left. In some urban areas, there are provisions which do away with the funeral altogether. This is what you can do in a number of American cities, for instance. You telephone a disposal organisation and an unmarked van arrives. The body is put into a plastic bag and taken off to a crematorium where it is burnt. You can have the ashes in a plastic box, if you want them. Or they are scattered somewhere. A bill is sent to you. All very convenient.

We are so accustomed to associate a person with his or her body that, even after death, the body retains great importance for us. Many have reported that a funeral service, in the absence of the body, seemed like a hollow mockery. Of course we know, logically, that after death the essential element – the element that makes a person a person – has gone, and that only the vehicle remains. But one cannot take farewell of a nebulous idea. There must be some concrete embodiment or physical symbol of the departed and this function is served by the body.

So, although different people have differing responses to the idea of viewing the face of the dead, before the coffin is closed, most are glad that they have done so, as, apart from any other factors, this forces one to accept positively what has happened and confirms that a time of separation has come. This may add to the pain, at the time, but, it does allow the process of recovery from grief to start from that moment.

Lily Pincus, a wise and experienced analyst, says in her book *Death and the Family*: 'Rituals express the collective unconscious of the culture, for which they perform a religious, social or *therapeutic* function. A funeral is one such ritual. It is a paying of respect, not to a dead body, but to the quality of the person who formerly inhabited that body, and to the part he or she played in the lives of those present. It is a positive confirmation to all that the death has occurred and an authorised focus for grief. It is a time for acceptance and for acknowledging that, for the bereaved, a new life has begun.'

## The Stages of Grief

Everyone who suffers bereavement goes through a number of well-recognised stages. These stages, although unpleasant, cannot be avoided or cut short if the normal, healthy process of recovery is to take place and you are to 'grow out of' your loss in both senses of the phrase.

Some of these stages are so painful, and seem to go on for so long, that you will feel sure that your agony will never end. But this is not so, and an account of the stages that millions have gone through before you, will, I hope, give you confidence that these stages *do* inevitably progress to a conclusion.

Although the stages are all matters of common experience, not every bereaved person goes through all of them. Some may appear to be omitted altogether, and the emphasis on particular stages varies considerably from person to person. So don't be concerned if you find that some of what follows doesn't seem to apply to you. You will certainly find that some of it does. None of these stages has to be complete before the next stars, or even occur in a fixed order, and some may be experienced throughout the whole mourning process.

### Shock

The stage of shock is almost universal and it features a kind of emotional numbness or anaesthesia, so that one may hardly feel anything at all. This may last for days and it may sometimes be well after the funeral before the emotions assert themselves again. People sometimes behave almost like automata during the stage of shock, carrying out important actions efficiently, with calm, impassive faces, and seeming to be unmoved by what has happened. Some, aware of their lack of emotion, even wonder, in an intellectual kind of way, whether they are not behaving callously.

Bereavement often resembles fear. This is understandable. Alarm and anxiety are very natural responses to the overturning of your whole world. Suddenly, all certainly and stability have gone, and you feel you can rely on nothing. We have seen how the body reacts to the shock and stress of the loss – with all the physical symptoms of fear – but there are also the longer-term psychological effects of loss of confidence in an orderly universe. Fear and anxiety make one jumpy, nervous and uncertain, and this may last for a long time. The recovery of confidence comes, not just from the passage of time, but by the eventual re-building of your life, either with a new partner or by acquiring, for yourself, the skills, knowledge, competence and motivation needed for full self-sufficiency.

### Searching

After every meaningful relationship, bereavement will feature searching and yearning. Habits, so deeply ingrained, cannot be shrugged off in an instant. When a person has been around for a long time, many of your reactions involve that person. So don't be surprised or embarrassed if you find yourself behaving as if the loved one is still around. This effect is so strong that, as we have seen, most bereaved people have hallucinations involving the dead person. These are not scary or ghostly, just a natural consequence of the fact that the deceased played such a large part in our lives.

### Anger

Anger, resentment and guilt are elements you must expect and live through. They are all natural and normal, and we have already seen how badly they can affect us if we do not clearly recognise that they are an almost universal feature of mourning, to be expected and properly managed. Anger defeats reason and so is dangerous. You must be wary of it. It is a damaging emotion – perhaps less damaging in bereavement, in which it often cannot be directed, than in marriage, in which it can – but capable of doing much harm to us. We have been hurt enough already without adding to the damage by our own angry or resentful acts.

### Depression

Depression, or sadness, is inevitable and is a consequence of loss of any kind. The greater the loss, the greater the reactive depression. And, of course, for many, the greatest loss they can sustain is the loss of a loved one. Again, sadness will not pass, merely as a result of the passage of time. It will only pass if and when the loss is made up, or replaced by something as valuable. Sometimes, the loss is too great to be borne – too great to make up. In such cases, the depression becomes a kind of illness – called pathological depression – which requires medical help. But even experts in the subject can do little more than help to support the sufferer until something comes along – or is sought out – to fill the great empty space in the damaged life.

### Acceptance

Eventually comes acceptance, and with it an easier mind. This is the necessary stage before new growth can occur, and it ought to involve a great deal of reminiscence about the dead person. The cure of mourning is *not* by forgetting. The person who has died is still an important part of ourselves and has contributed to the personalities we shall carry to the end of our own lives. So reminiscence helps us to look at those aspects of ourselves which derive from the other. As we grow, under the altered circumstances, we may have to alter opinions or attitudes, in the light of new knowledge and understanding, and there is no harm in this. We must never, out of respect for the dead, try to hold on to opinions we now know are wrong. For if we try to do this, we shall be seriously interfering with our progress to the last stage of bereavement – growth.

## The Recovery of Christine Parsons

The Parsons had been known as the 'ideal' married couple and they were certainly deeply devoted to one another. Neither of them made any secret, to their friends, of the fact that each felt incomplete without the other. John was a successful banker, almost ten years older than Christine, and she had regularly sought his advice on all sorts of practical and financial matters. He, in his turn, deferred to her on all aesthetic matters and acknowledged her supremacy in literature and arts. Each took a close interest in the other's concerns and their conversations were endless. Their sexual life was active and fully satisfying, but they had had no children.

'I'm only half a person without John,' Christine would say, 'I wouldn't dream of making an important decision without consulting him.'

'The same goes for me,' John would add, 'My life would be a very drab business without that girl.'

John Parsons died, without warning, when he was only forty-nine. He drove off to his Head Office one morning, and just before lunch, Christine had a phone call to say that he had had a stroke and was unconscious. Soon after admission to hospital he died and the post-mortem examination showed that he had had a massive sub-arachnoid haemorrhage from a brain aneurysm.

Christine went into a state of acute shock and, for three or four days, would make no response to anyone, not even to her closest friends. John's younger sister Catriona, a professional temping secretary who was devoted to Christine, moved in with her the day John died – 'Just to make sure she was all right' – and was, at first, hurt by her apparent coldness and rejection of sympathy. Catriona, too, was mourning John and felt that the shared grief should bring them closer together. But Christine would say nothing and Catriona had no idea of what was going on in her mind.

The state of shock broke at the grave-side and, as the coffin was lowered, Christine turned blindly to Catriona, weeping bitterly and with her arms held out in a mute appeal for comfort. After that, the two women were much closer together and did, to some extent, comfort one another. But whereas Catriona continued in a state of profound sadness, Christine moved into a restless phase in which guilt alternated with anger, sometimes expressed even as resentment against John. During the early days, she seemed more physically active than before, constantly jumping up and going into another room or running upstairs for no obvious reason. Catriona knew she was searching for John.

Christine spoke freely about her emotions:

'I lie awake at night, alone and abandoned, terribly aware of the empty place beside me, and going over and over in my mind how I'm going to manage. I'm longing for comfort and it has been taken away. It's like a constant physical pain. And I can't help feeling that it's all his fault. I know it's illogical and totally unreasonable, but there's this resentment that he did this to me. He knew how important he was to me and how I depended on him – and still he left me. And then I try to be more logical and realise that I can't blame John and that this is God's will, and I hate God. And then I have a dreadful guilt feeling, both about this and about whether I failed John in some way – maybe I should have noticed that there was something wrong with him. He couldn't have had such a serious condition without there being some indication, and if I didn't notice it who would? He did have headaches, sometimes, and I never took them seriously . . .'

Catriona often heard Christine speaking when she was alone and she soon realised that her sister in law was still reacting as if John continued to live in the house with them. Several times, she heard her cry out, in a matter-of-fact tone 'What was that you said, love?' and quite often Christine spoke as if John were still around. Comments such as, 'I'm pretty sure John won't approve of that!'

The yearning and searching went on for weeks, and with them the anger.

'Why John?' she asked, over and over again, in a tone of bitterness and resentment, 'Why me?'

Christine seemed to be searching for a focus for her anger.

John's death had been so sudden and was so obviously not the fault of anyone, that she could find no one to blame expect God. But her belief in God was vague and nebulous and she could not do this with any real conviction. So she was inclined to turn her anger against the nearest person – Catriona – and this produced a very ambivalent state of mind and some suggestions so unreasonable that Catriona's patience was tried to the limit.

'Very convenient for you, I suppose, being able to live here, indefinitely, rent-free – free food, too – doing nothing . . .'

Catriona pushed the dinner she had prepared into the oven and banged the door.

'OK', she said, cuttingly, 'If that's really how you feel, we can do one of two things. Either I buzz off or I pay you. Do let me know which you prefer.' She was thinking how she had let her flat go and that she would certainly have to pay a much higher rent for the same kind of accommodation. 'Better make up your mind.' she said.

Christine slid off the kitchen stool and put her arms round her sister-in-law. 'I don't know why I say these things,' she said, contritely. 'I just have this terrible urge to get at someone, or something . . .'

Almost from the beginning, Christine had wanted to talk about John, and Catriona had been happy to oblige her. To begin with, Christine could say nothing that was not highly complimentary. She seemed to want to canonize her former husband. For a time Catriona went along with this, but one day she said, 'You're trying to make out he was a saint. You know that's not so.'

There was a long pause, and then Christine smiled a little and said, 'No, of course he wasn't. Just a very nice guy.'

'Sure.'

It was as if Christine had been given permission to end a formal stage in her mourning. Almost at once she became more open and frank and soon her frankness about John and about their relationship was surprising Catriona.

'It's actually quite a relief for me to be able to tell someone about my blighted career –'

'What do you mean?' asked Catriona, 'Are you talking about your magazine articles? I thought you'd done rather well with these. I knew John was frightfully proud of you.'

'I was offered a full-time job working on an enormous encyclopaedia of art . . .' Christine mentioned a leading London publisher.

'Good heavens! What a marvellous opportunity! Why didn't you take it?'

Christine hesitated, then said, 'John didn't want me to.'

'Why not, for heaven's sake?'

'It sounds improbable, but he was actually terrified that I would reach some kind of independence.'

'The so-and-so!'

'It wasn't just financial independence he was worried about. He was really scared that if I got into an absorbing job, with challenge and excitement, I would be less interested in him.'

'Actually, this all figures. I often wondered how you had managed to change John so much. Now I realise you hadn't.'

'No, not fundamentally.'

'Was he jealous of other men?'

'Oh, I never gave him the slightest reason to be. But I know that if I had taken the job, he would have been deeply worried about the people I worked with. I expect it would have ruined our marriage.'

'What on earth did he say? I mean, when you told him about the offer.'

He just went deathly pale and looked at me.'

'Didn't say anything?'

'No. Just waited for me to make the obvious comment –'

'That he didn't like the idea?'

'Yes.'

'Which comment you duly made?'

'Of course.'

'And he said?'

'He would be sorry to think that I didn't find my present life satisfying enough. That a hobby was one thing, a profession another. That he would find it difficult to carry on without my support at home. That his income was amply sufficient. Etc. etc. etc.'

'So you gave up the idea, completely?'

'Pretty resentfully – but, yes.'

'And you feel you've been unfulfilled?'

'Well, that's right. No kids, no career. Just a few years of acting as a kind of acolyte to John.'

There was a pause, then Catriona said, 'There is, of course, another obvious comment . . .'

'Quite. Now's my chance.'

## Loneliness

Loneliness after bereavement is very common and, sadly, it is often the most severely bereaved who are liable to be the most lonely. These are usually people most dependent on another, people whose lives have been completely bound up in that of their spouse or partner and have had no inclination, or opportunity, to seek a wide circle of acquaintance. This is especially so with elderly people, and the loneliness may be especially poignant if bereavement occurs soon after retired people have moved to a new area to enjoy together the house they had long dreamed of. The one left will indeed be a stranger in a stranger land.

Another reason for loneliness is the tendency for friends and acquaintances actually to avoid a bereaved person. There are several reasons for this, but it is chiefly because people seek the company of others for the reward they get from the association. Human intercourse has to be a two-way process to succeed – both have to give. But the bereaved person is temporarily incapable of giving, only of taking, and however sympathetic others may feel, it is difficult to keep up a relationship with someone who is deeply preoccupied with his or her own miseries, and is angry, depressed and perhaps guilty.

However you try, as a bereaved person you are likely to drive others away, especially during the first few weeks when things are at their worst and when, although you may be confused in your wants, you need people most.

But loneliness is not just the absence of people in general. The bitterest loneliness is the absence of the beloved with whom so much was shared which has now become meaningless – the absence of a proper emotional association. If the relationship has been particularly close, it may seem impossible that any other relationship could ever replace it. Standards have been set which no other person is capable of meeting. And because what is needed is a mature rapport, and such a thing is so difficult to find, at that stage, it is common for bereaved people to come to believe that there is no one in the world who could ever relieve the loneliness.

Children, whether small or grown-up, do not provide an adequate substitute for the person lost. Children have their own concerns and do not provide the kind of emotional relationships necessary to relieve loneliness. Also, small children can take up so much time that the bereaved person is deprived of the chance to form a new and worth-while relationship.

You have probably recognised that close relatives and married friends, however kind and helpful, do not provide what is needed to relieve your emotional loneliness. You may find the pressure for relief becoming so strong that you may take up with someone you recognise as unsuitable. Or you may even find yourself in a humiliating situation, through being unable to restrain the expression of your need. Mistakes and damage to the sense of self-respect are likely.

So, whenever you think the time is right, and that should be sooner rather than later, you must get yourself involved in some kind of group activity. Evening or daytime classes, groups, clubs, bowling, church work, voluntary aid – there is no end to the possibilities. Or you could consider taking up a job involving association with others. The world is full of lonely people and the tragedy is that so many of them go on for so long without finding each other.

# RECOVERY FROM MOURNING

The recovery from mourning is not a process of forgetting, for one cannot, and should not, forget something that has been such a vital part of one's life for so long. Of course there will inevitably be some forgetting and this will always bring regret and even, sometimes, guilt. Those who advise you to try to forget the past show a lack of insight into the nature of your feelings which you are likely to find upsetting.

Dougal MacPhie recovered consciousness in hospital. He had 30 per cent burns and multiple fractures and was in terrible pain. When it was thought he was fit enough to stand the news, a young House Surgeon went in to tell him that him that his wife and two children were dead – killed in the same gas explosions that had so seriously injured him. The doctor was inexperienced and full of sympathy. As Dougal was desperately trying to assimilate the terrible truth, he said:

'You'll get over it, old chap,' he said, 'Just try to put it all behind you. Forget the past and try to get on with your life.'

For months afterwards, Dougal could not get this advice out of his mind. It had been given at a time when he was critically sensitive to anything he was told, and it made a powerful impression on him. Time and again, afterwards, he said:

'How can I do that? I dinna want to forget them. They're all I have. I canna forget them. I jist want them back.'

People who have been cut in half don't want to forget the half they have lost. It is a part of themselves and must be retained until something can gradually be put in its place. The difficulty is worst for the elderly who have been married a long time and who have been so dependent on each other that they have become like one person. Such people are often too old, and too set in their ways, to be able to compensate or to do much to fill the gap.

So the first point about recovery is that as much of the past as possible should be retained. Take what comfort you can from your memories. Cherish them. The dead person is inside you, unchanging. Lily Pincus, founder of the Tavistock Institute for Marital Studies, shared with her husband eleven years of the knowledge that he was dying. After he died, she gave her husband's clothes to a young colleague of her husband's, of similar build, and for years afterwards she would recognise, 'with a pang of pleasure' the well-remembered clothes on the other man.

The next stage is to recognise the painful fact that you have to rebuild your life anew. The life that has been damaged by your bereavement contained much that closely involved the person you have lost. Much of your shared experience has shaped you and many of your opinions and attitudes have, consciously or otherwise, been formed by that other person. It may seem to you impossible that you will ever be interested in anything again, for in the past, interest has always led to comment to the other, perhaps argument, modification of opinion, growth.

Interest is one of the most valuable commodities you have and without it you will stay where you are. Interest *must* be cultivated at all cost, for it is only through interest that your life will be able to go forward. Do not ever feel that you are being unfaithful if you find that there is a small stirring of interest in something new and unconnected with your lost loved one. It is your right to go on with your life and this is the only way you can.

Of course, if you can begin to take an interest in something which *did* concern your loved one, so much the better. Many widows have derived great comfort and consolation from taking over and continuing some work, or business, in which the husband had been engaged. If this could possibly apply to you, consider it seriously, however unlikely it may seem that you could succeed. You will certainly be feeling pessimistic and you may well be convinced that such activities are quite beyond you. But it may be that it is only the depression arising from your present unhappy condition that makes it seem that way.

Interest starts your mind working along new lines and helps you to break out of the short-circuited loops you have been in since your loss. Interest restarts the process of mind-building – the re-synthesis of the missing part of your life. The younger you are, the easier this will be. There are several reasons for this. For a start, you are likely to have spent less time with the loved one than has an older person, and the effect of the association on your total personality will be less. Your mind and character will be less formed than that of an older person, and will have greater scope for further development. And, however you may feel to the contrary, it is certainly true that younger people are, in general, more resilient and adaptable than the elderly.

So the commonly expressed idea, that bereavement in the young is more tragic than in the old, is wrong. The truth is that the older the bereaved person, the greater the loss and the graver the problem of recovery. Many older people never enjoy any degree of recovery from bereavement – may never want to – and it is common for one spouse to die soon after the death of the first.

## The Need for Human Contact

The most potent reliever of the pains of grief is empathy, and you should clearly understand this term. The word empathy is often used wrongly, as if it merely meant 'sympathy'. Now empathy certainly involves sympathy but this is a *consequence* of empathy. Empathy is the state existing between two people when one of them recognises that he or she is able, however briefly, to feel as another person does, to be able to adopt an identical outlook, even to share identical emotions. Continuing, long-term empathy, particularly if reciprocated, is called love.

Sympathy is different. Here, the sympathising person is largely concerned with his or her own response and feelings and is not seriously concerned with the reality of the other person's internal experience. So the other person merely becomes a kind of mirror in which the sympathiser can study his or her own reaction. The sufferer is thus, in a sense, insulated from the sympathiser.

Now you cannot, of course, assume that empathy will automatically be available to you. What you can do is to place yourself in a position in which you yourself, by providing empathy, can reasonably expect it in return. And the way you do this is to get in touch with someone recently bereaved, like yourself, who will know what you are going through and who, if willing, will be readily able to empathize with you.

In Britain, one way to do this is through the medium of CRUSE – BEREAVEMENT CARE, the wonderful organisation dedicated to all those – not only widows – who have been bereaved and are suffering. Cruse has counsellors in all areas of Britain and it is likely you will be able to benefit from direct counselling, by letter, telephone or in your own home. But counsellors are usually very busy people, many with heavy professional or business responsibilities of their own and the time they can devote to any one case is necessarily limited.

So, as well as offering an immense amount of invaluable practical advice and confidential support, CRUSE – BEREAVEMENT CARE can put you in touch with other people in your position with whom you can spend as much time as is mutually agreeable. It is so much easier to see what is wrong with someone else's attitude or approach to a problem than it is to see what is wrong with your own. This is one important reason why you need help at a time of bereavement and one good reason why meeting others of your own kind who are suffering in the same way as you are, can be so valuable. Similar organisations are available in many countries – your doctor may be able to advise you.

Talk is therapeutic. Talk about the deceased, about your own feelings, about your worries and fears. But talk is also very revealing to others and if you can enter into an empathic relationship with someone else you can become each other's counsellor. Of course you will make mistakes. There will be misunderstandings, embarrassments, emotional upset. But this kind of communication is infinitely to be preferred to the loneliness and despair of solitary hopelessness in grief. Many have found in it, the very relief they so desperately needed. Many have formed new and important relationships and permanent friends. Some have found remarriage.

Empathic positive relationships of this kind call for sensitivity, patience and understanding, and not all possess these qualities. It is essential that each should be clearly aware of the nature of the other's feelings. These feelings must be respected and never criticised. Careful thought should be given before any comment is made on the other's behaviour, even if that behaviour is seen clearly to be destructive, negative or damaging. Comments must be kind, fully considered and constructive. It's no good criticising adversely unless a realistic and healthy alternative can immediately be proposed. And it is hopeless to go at the other like a bull at a gate on an early acquaintance. Nothing but sympathy should be expressed at the first meeting and your reactions should be noted so that they may be fully considered before the next – if there is a next.

Fairness and mutuality are of the essence. You have to take as well as to give. And do avoid harping on the other's obvious weaknesses. It is much more constructive to emphasise strengths.

# 8 Children and Bereavement

## THE CHILD'S CONCEPT OF DEATH_____

The child's idea of death comes from observation of how grown-ups react to death. This is how children acquire emotional reactions, and these can be good or bad, depending on what they observe of our reactions. Logic has nothing to do with it. The child draws inferences, which may be very powerful, simply from seeing how we react. This is an important point for those dealing with older children who are dying. Such children may be terrified by indications that we are horrified or even severely distressed.

Children between about three and five have no concept of the finality of death. They see death as a departure, probably temporary, and, unless they have been frightened by thoughtless adults, have no sense of the gravity of the situation. They do, of course, suffer exactly the same kind of pain as anyone else, from the loss of someone precious to them. But they do not anticipate their own deaths in terms of loss, as adults often do. I shall have more to say about this important point later, when dealing with bereaved children.

Around eight or nine, children come to an adult understanding of death and an awareness that it comes to all of us. The attitude taken to death varies considerably, depending on the early experience of adult reactions, and may be very good or very bad. Thoughtless exposure of a child, of any age, to the grief or distress of others, or allowing a young child to attend a funeral without a full explanation of what is happening, can be damaging. So, too, can refusal to discuss the subject of death. The child cannot understand what has happened but will always be acutely aware that something very important is going on. Refusal to discuss it, or even deflection of the child's questions, establishes a strong taboo – a sense that the subject is forbidden, mysterious, prohibited – which will remain with the child for the rest of its life.

Children, like adults, need to be allowed to express their distress and sense of loss when a parent dies. Shared mourning is best, but you may find this difficult if you are not prepared to face up to the need for a frank and open discussion on what has happened. This, as we shall see, is an essential part of the handling of a child's grief. You should understand that if the grief is not allowed to show itself in the normal and natural way, it will come out in other ways – in moodiness, aggressive or resentful behaviour, sometimes lying or stealing, and in physical symptoms.

We have seen that mourning must be worked through and completed. But the 'stiff upper lip' syndrome, so beloved of the English, may prevent this. And even in a child, the failure to complete mourning may result in persistent depression and other ill effects. Children mourn naturally and will do so if allowed. But the blunting of emotion, which you may experience for a long time after the bereavement, and your own difficulty in expressing your grief, may confuse them – perhaps lead them to think that you do not care. This is just one of the many difficulties you have to face when left with young children.

You are likely to feel that very young children are too young to understand what you say to them. This may be so, but something is likely to get through. If the child does not understand, no harm is done, but the very act of talking about the death is valuable and if the child observes your grief, he or she will share it.

## BEREAVED CHILDREN

The effect of the loss of a parent is, in general, the more serious the younger the child at the time of the parent's death or departure. This will not surprise anyone with even a basic understanding of the nature of the child-parent relationship and its importance for the vital early conditioning – consider it as programming, if you like – of the child. Much has been published on the subject, and it is known that children bereaved at an early age, quite often grow up into adults with a low opinion of themselves, chronic worriers who regularly suffer strong guilt feelings and are given to depression and anxiety.

This kind of personality damage is obviously one of the worst things that can happen to anyone and it is important to consider whether anything can be done to reduce the risk. Unfortunately, in most cases, the only person available to help the child is the bereaved adult. If you are in such a position you are likely to feel that knowledge of this kind is just too much of an additional burden for you to bear. But I would like to suggest that there is at least a possibility that accepting this responsibility might even provide you with some comfort.

## What Do You Say To The Child?

'Peter was two and a half when his father died. By then he had quite a good vocabulary of single words and was just starting to string them together into sentences. Suddenly, just at that point, the process stopped and he seemed to regress. It was a whole year before he uttered anything more than single words. His first sentence was, "Where is my Daddy?"'

How does one respond to a question like that? It is difficult enough to try to find an answer without having to translate it into terms an infant can understand. For many, the immediate impulse is to lie – to find some comforting formula to help one out of the difficulty. 'Daddy's gone away.' Something of that sort. Others may allow their anger against God to colour their response. 'Jesus came and took him to Heaven.' or 'God called him, and he went.'

These responses, although very common and understandable, are neither helpful nor desirable. If Daddy decided to go away, it means that he didn't care and this could play havoc with a child's confidence and self-image. It might also raise the possibility that Mummy might also decide to 'go away.'

The first thing to remember is that your young child sees itself as the centre of the universe and frequently believes that anything that goes wrong is his or her fault. Most children are thoroughly familiar with the concept of blame long before they can possibly understand the concept of death. They get this idea from you, for you would be less than human if you had never, at least occasionally, expressed disapproval. In the midst of many mysteries, children try desperately to make some kind of sense of cause and effect and regularly postulate magical connections. So you must assume the definite possibility that the child will blame himself or herself for the death – and you will not handle this by telling lies.

But talking about death to children need not be as difficult as you think. Probably, your instinct will be to shy away from discussion of death. A colleague, with whom I discussed this point, recounted how, when she was about ten years old, she once saw that the much younger children, from next door, were looking curiously at a dead bird. They asked her why it was unable to move, so she tried to explain to them what death was. She told them that it happened to everyone, 'but not for a long time – not until they were old.' The children were very interested and the discussion led to their playing games in which they pretended to be dead. There was no content of horror or distress, only a pleasing *frisson* of half-alarm.

Unfortunately, the sequel to the episode was a sharp note of protest from the parents of these children requesting that my friend should not frighten the children with such morbid matters. To children, there is nothing morbid or unhealthy in the idea of death; it was the response of the parents that was unhealthy.

So do not, on that account, he inhibited from talking frankly to your child about the real reason for the absence of the beloved parent. Children readily accept authoritative statements, so you must be careful what you say. To the best of your ability and the child's understanding, you must make it perfectly clear that the death was involuntary, unwished, and in no circumstances the responsibility of any living person. You must emphasise that the dead parent did not wish to go and was very sorry to leave the family, but had no choice in the matter. But you must also try to mitigate distress on behalf of the deceased by explaining that the dead person cannot now feel grief. Perhaps, above all, you must show, by word and deed, that the event has in no way diminished your love and concern for the child.

None of this will be easy, and you may feel that you already have enough to cope with. But it is important. Careful studies by experienced psychiatrists have shown that the effects of the death of a parent on the social and educational development and happiness of a child can be markedly affected by the way the child is handled immediately afterwards. And one of the most important factors in avoiding these unhappy effects is open and frank discussion of what has happened.

Dr Dora Black, a psychiatrist who has specialised in this subject, has reported that when parents were counselled on how to handle this situation, the effects on the children were that there were fewer and briefer behaviour problems, that there was less trouble with sleeping and restlessness, and their general health was better and that they had fewer problems with eduction. Such children found it easier than others to cry over, and to talk freely about, the dead parent.

Here is what a girl of sixteen wrote about her father, who died when she was eleven. 'The only thing that I find difficult is the way other people react ... Really I would love to talk about my Dad for hours on end, but I never have because nobody wants to know. They seem to think that is wrong.'

# DEATH OF A CHILD

No one who has not experienced it can ever know what the death of a child means to the bereaved. For many, it is the most terrible loss suffered in the whole of their lives. Others seem to be able to assimilate it and live on, apparently unchanged. The overall response seems to differ in different countries and cultures. In America, for instance, the loss of a child is regarded as a less serious blow than it is in Israel, where the death of a child is considered by many to be more serious than the death of a spouse. Studies done at the Hadassah Medical Centre in Jerusalem have shown that bereaved parents, even five years after the death of the child, often continued to suffer emotional disturbance.

There is some comfort in the knowledge that young children do not think of their own deaths. The stage of development of the higher brain functions makes it impossible, in the early years of life, for them to have any realistic concept of death. And even up to the age of eight or nine they are not able to grasp the idea of the permanent ending of their own lives. So when young children die, although the loss and the grief may be dreadful to the bereaved, at least there is the consolation that the child suffered none of the fears and terrors which some older people have to face. We, all of us, at the last, die easily, in exactly the same way as we fall asleep, but in the case of young children there is the additional fact that, even well before the final stages, they have no idea of what is happening. So we need not be distressed on their account, unless, as we have seen, we are unable to hide our own distress from them.

The real burden falls on you – the bereaved parent – and a grievous burden it is. We know that, for many, the loss of a child is a more severe blow and has more serious emotional consequences than the loss of a husband, wife or parent. We know that, while the death of a child may bring the grieving parents closer together, it may often have the opposite effect and that separation is not uncommon. The gravity of the loss, of course, varies and we must recognise that some children are more precious than others.

Here is a touching account, by a woman who, although married, had to work, alone, through her grief over the death of her son.

### Daniel's Death

'Daniel had cystic fibrosis and, as I knew, a lot of children died from it. But I didn't realise how close he was to dying until the last minute.

He was just six. He actually went into hospital to be started off on a new diet for cystic children. I thought it was worth trying and I persuaded the Consultant to try it to see if it would help him to get his strength back again. So they decided to control it by having him in hospital. He went in, and started on the diet, but within the first week he caught a chest infection and went quite rapidly downhill. I don't know if he knew what was happening – I think he suspected.

'It wasn't something we had talked about. I hadn't talked to him about dying, but we had talked about how unfair it was that he was ill. He said, "Why me?" I would agree with him. I just said, "No, it's not fair. Life isn't always fair and sometimes it's dreadful." There's not much else you can say under the circumstances. He used to say "Why aren't I like everybody else?" He was at a normal school, but he had a bad chest and couldn't run like everybody else. There were many things he couldn't do. He had lots of chest infections and needed constant physiotheraphy – had to be bashed around. That's no fun for a child.

'I hadn't realised that he was actually dying until the last couple of days, when he went into a coma. Up to then there had been so many scares that I had got used to it. I just hadn't realised and then I suddenly was embroiled in it. One of the few doctors who managed to talk to me said, "Has he ever talked to you about death?" The doctors were all too ... they are very good when there is something they can do, but when they can't do anything to help, very few of them know how to be, somehow. Particularly with a child. This was an acute children's ward, but you don't expect children to die that often under your care. And so we were in a side ward and very few people came anywhere near us.

'Doctors aren't perfect. There's a sort of conspiracy between doctors and people to make doctors into Gods with the power of life and death. If one has given a doctor this God-like power and he fails – has not kept the loved one alive – then obviously you're going to be furious with them. It's sad for the doctors, because they do get a lot of anger from the bereaved. Doctors are not necessarily any better at dealing with emotional things than the rest of us – some of them are a good deal worse. I got a lot more support from the other parents around the ward because I slept there the last two nights and there was a great deal of solidarity.

'Daniel's Consultant ran in for about a minute and said, "We have decided, on balance, that he shouldn't be put on a ventilator." In other words – they were going to let him die. I thought, wouldn't it have been natural if he could have discussed that with us, rather than just announcing his decision. But the *other* paediatric Consultant – and Daniel wasn't his patient – came and sat with me. So I was able to say things to him like "How long is this going to be and is it going to hurt? Is he going to suffer? Can I *bear* it?" That sort of thing. It was very helpful. He didn't need to do that – he just came in and sat, a couple of times. We weren't even under his care. I have a notion that doctors are just trained to act – whereas a lot of what is needed in these cases is just *being* there. Doctors are not always very good at dealing with emotion. Some of the older ones are better.

'The other parents were very supportive – we were all in the same boat. If you are going through something as dreadful as that – so fundamentally awful as having a child of yours die – actually living in that sort of atmosphere – an awful lot of the normal reserve and nonsense with which we surround ourselves is stripped away. There is no time for that sort of thing, and so you meet much more directly and more honestly – and that is supportive in itself. There is none of the peripheral rubbish with which we defend ourselves most of the time. I was only there for two nights – some of them were there for much longer. A lot of children had been in there for a long time with liver disease. Some of the parents knew each other very well. I met one of the parents later, by chance, at the zoo, and we had a long talk on a bench. Her little child had died, too.

'Daniel was in a coma and didn't recover. Afterwards there were hundreds of things I wished I could have said and done. I wished he hadn't died in hospital. I wished I had had the nerve to bring him home – so many regrets afterwards. I wish I'd taken on board fully the fact that he was dying and had had the nerve to take him home. I probably wouldn't have been brave enough and I might have felt guilty for not giving him hospital care if he had been at home. But at the time it was so awful that . . .

'I was there when he died. It was towards evening and he'd been in a deep coma all day. He was in an oxygen tent into which they were pumping mist to try to loosen his chest. His pyjamas got awfully wet so we decided to change them and I think it was moving him to do that which actually precipitated the last moment. I had been terrified that he would actually gasp and struggle for breath and I didn't think I could take that – I had been terribly brave up to then. Occasionally I had a little cry. I remember an awful nurse coming in and saying "What are you doing crying, dear?" Quite extraordinary! I think it's a total denial – some of them are so young they've no idea what that sort of thing is like. I said, "Why do you think I'm crying?

I'm crying because my son is dying." She very wisely turned on her heel and went away.

'So when he died, there was me, my husband and an agency nurse in the background. I was holding his hand and he just struggled a little bit and tried to take a breath – you could see that he hadn't absorbed any oxygen because his face flushed very red and then he took another breath soon afterwards. Nothing came from that and he just didn't breath again. It was very quick and he didn't struggle or suffer. He was very down and, I think, completely unapproachable. I mean, I talked to him and held his hand, but I don't think he heard anything. I don't know.'

'I was worried about whether I was going to manage it or break down completely and collapse. I think I didn't cry until I got home. I was extremely together, which I regret in a way. We stopped for some petrol on the way home and I remember thinking – "My son died, and here I am, buying petrol." It was extraordinary – completely unreal. We had to go back the next day to the hospital. I was angry with the Consultant. He had said he would see us, but I said "No, we don't want to see him". I do understand the doctors' difficulties. It's difficult for anybody to be up against the raw emotions, and if you are a sensitive and open doctor, you are laying yourself open to it every day of the week. You have to be detached to some extent, but, at the same time, you shouldn't be denying your own emotions to such an extent that you can't recognise them. There are emotional needs as well as physical needs, but in most acute wards I don't think they are catered for. I certainly felt the lack. I needed someone to talk to – there wasn't anyone. We were left alone.

'My younger son, Joe, was just three at the time and so I was forever rushing between home and the hospital and the traffic jams were intolerable. It was ghastly because I thought he might die before I got back. We were completely honest with him. We told him, when we got back from hospital, that his brother had died. He didn't really know what it meant. He came down the next morning and said "I dreamed Daniel died." We said, "It wasn't a dream – it was for real."

I decided he shouldn't go to the funeral, so my neighbour had him. But I took him up to the grave quite soon afterwards, and we took up a whole lot of pansies in pots and he helped me plant them. That was very good. He was *tremendously* pleased about that. He didn't react in any particular way about it until quite a few months afterwards when he did the same thing twice – a devastating wrecking of the bedroom. They had shared the same bedroom I went up one night and he had totally wrecked the entire bedroom with a little friend who was staying. Every poster was pulled off the wall, every box of toys was emptied out. You couldn't get across the room. He said it was because all the things around the walls were Daniel's. It was just devastating . . .

'I don't know exactly what the meaning of it was, but it was linked to Daniel – to the fact that he wasn't there any more, and Joe wanted to get away from the memories . . . I've talked to him about it since, but he can't remember why he did it. He just knew he had to do it. He did it twice. There may have been some anger but it wasn't as simple as that. I think it was multi-determined, really. It didn't worry me.

'I can't remember all the details of the last days, now. I used to remember *all* the details – exactly what happened and when. For a couple of months after the death I really needed to talk about it. Everyone had heard it once through, or there wasn't anyone I wanted to tell it to, so I used to tell it to myself. I wrote it down. I actually used to talk out loud in the bath at night, and imagine I was being interviewed. It was a reworking, over and over, so that I could gradually detach myself. For about a year afterwards I used to be depressed every Thursday – the day he died.

'There are certain of my friends around here who never mentioned that Daniel had died. I was outraged. Although there was a little bit of me that knew it was difficult for them to know what to say, the fact that something so appalling as the death of a child could occur and not even be mentioned – seemed to me completely outrageous! I was furious with the few who didn't mention it.

'For about ten days it was so easy to talk. I felt stripped naked. All my usual defences were gone and I felt I could be completely direct with people – and it was really good, wonderful. I knew it wouldn't last, that it would all build up again, but it never built up completely. A lot of friends were wonderful. Some would just arrive with a bottle of wine and sit around the kitchen table and talk about him. They were there, and would talk if you wanted to and not if you didn't – that was really good.

'But in a way, his death was also a relief. It's horrible seeing a child suffer and to begin to realise that he won't get better. And then there was the sheer worry of looking after him, constantly listening to his cough – wondering how serious it was, whether it was another infection and whether one should phone the doctor. Frankly, it was a relief not to have the worry any more of looking after a very sick child.

'I did miss him, though, because he was absolutely *smashing* – he was gorgeous! One day I came down and saw his scooter in the hall and was hit with a *wave* of missing him. I've still got the last things he wore tucked away in the bottom of a drawer and sometimes I cry, as you can see. It isn't as if I haven't mourned him. I have done a lot of crying. It will always be there. Grief isn't a well you let out once and for all. I think it is bad for people who don't express their grief. I don't cry and cry any more. I just feel sad when I think of him.

'When Daniel died my husband had a hard time coping. He still cries when he talks about him. It is a shame that we each had to grieve in our own separate ways. We had been having problems with our marriage before we knew Daniel was going to die, and so we couldn't help each other very much. Now he has remarried and it's wonderful for him that he recently had a baby girl.

'After Daniel's death I decided to go away for a while with Joe, the young one, and stay with my sister. Some people would say that this is running away, but I felt it was a great help. Of course, all the feelings are there to be gone through again, when you come back. I never took any sleeping pills – I never had any difficulty in sleeping, I was so exhausted. After Daniel died, I gave up the course I had been taking. My husband was quite angry. But I had got behind when I was looking after Daniel, and I was so tired.

'I needed that extra year off. Then, when I started to study again, I took a different course which wasn't so much fun, but it was a serious and full course of study which gave me the qualifications for my present profession.

'I do think that mourning and the ritual of mourning are important. A while ago when I was in Switzerland I heard a single bell tolling very slowly. Then the bells in all the other valleys all around joined in, one by one, and everyone knew there had been a death. I should like to have done something like that for Daniel.

'I didn't let Joe see me crying very much. But later he said that I should have let him share my grief. Recently, when a friend had died, Abe – now seventeen – found me crying by the telephone and comforted me. I think he was glad to be able to talk.

'Daniel had a close friend, a little girl, who was very fond of him. After he died, she used to come and see me. She brought me flowers and used to talk about him. She said once that I was the only person who knew how she felt. We are still good friends. About a year later, her father painted a picture of Daniel and gave it to me. It is very good. I can remember so many things about Daniel and I can enjoy them, in spite of his suffering. He *was* a lovely child.

'One thing happened that comforted me. For years I had always felt bad on Daniel's birthday, but now a very good friend of mine has had a baby on the very same day – so now his birthday has another meaning. I was already a godmother to the sister. Somehow, this helps to cancel out the power of my sorrow on that day.'

## Miscarriage and Stillbirth

This, too, is in every sense a bereavement, although those who have not experienced it may not think so. Almost all women who suffer stillbirth, miscarriage, or even, to a lesser extent, early abortion, go through a period of mourning. This is easy to understand in the case of loss of a baby late in pregnancy. In that case, the baby is already an individual who may have been given a name, who has been felt moving, both by the mother and the father and who, quite often, has been ascribed a personality of its own. The parents feelings of possession and kinship are already strong and their expectations, for the future, bright.

But even in the case of a much smaller foetus, emotional factors connected with one's attitudes to life and relationships are often stronger than one might expect and very few women are able to contemplate the loss of a tiny baby – even if the abortion has been deliberately sought – with indifference.

The effects of miscarriage and, particularly, stillbirth are often severe and may last for a very long time. It is common for the mother to mourn for over a year. In the case of the father the period of mourning is usually less – generally about six months. The loss of a baby often puts a heavy strain on the relationship of the parents and this is usually because the couple fail to share their grief. Quite often, the father seems to think that he should be very controlled and unemotional, and this leads the mother to think that he is uncaring. The death of a baby is the apparent cause of marital separation in about six per cent of cases. I say 'apparent' because the evidence suggests that in such cases there are usually other problems. Happily, for most, such an event has the opposite effect and serves to bring couples closer together.

Unfortunately, the situation is often made worse by the well-meaning but misguided behaviour of medical and nursing staff at the time of the event. There is, for instance, a widespread belief that it would be unnecessarily distressing, and perhaps even damaging, to the parents to see the dead baby. As a result, the baby is taken away and disposed of without the parents knowing what happens to him. The causes of death, too, are often thought to be too painful to disclose. Strangulation by the umbilical cord, displaced placenta, diabetes in the mother, acquired congenital abnormalities, hereditary diseases, rhesus incompatibility – whatever the cause, a full explanation is thought by some medical people as likely merely to add to the grief of the parents.

These views are mostly wrong. When parents have never seen or touched their baby, they tend to feel he has never existed. They have feelings of great emptiness and commonly suffer prolonged depression because of their inability to grieve for a 'real' infant. Informed medical opinion is now greatly in favour of encouraging parents to hold the dead baby and to ask detailed questions about the cause of death. Inappropriate guilt feelings about the latter are very common and these can only be finally put to rest by a full medical explanation.

A careful study of this problem was made in 1978 by a group of medical and nursing specialists. The group included midwives, obstetricians, paediatricians, and psychiatrists and the result of their study was to make some clear recommendations. They agreed that parents should see and hold the dead baby, that the baby should be named, that a formal funeral should be held in which the parents should take part, that the causes of death should be fully discussed and explained, and that any implications for future pregnancies should be made entirely clear.

It was believed that if these recommendations were followed, the normal bereavement reactions would be possible and that, in time, full recovery would result.

Most women who have had a miscarriage or still-birth experience a strong desire to have another baby and about half of them are pregnant again within about a year. But there is plenty of evidence that women suffer much anxiety about, and sometimes adverse reactions to the 'replacement baby'. If you are in this situation, it is imperative that you have good and understanding medical advice.

## Abortion

It may seem odd to include an account of a woman's reaction to an abortion in this chapter, and many would point out that abortion is a wilful act, quite different in its nature from the involuntary loss normally thought of as bereavement. Even so, the element of bereavement, in abortion, is not negligible. Although, for most, the element of loss in abortion is quite a minor matter compared to the loss of a baby or a late miscarriage, women are often surprised by the strength of their own reactions.

One of the women interviewed for this book had decided to have an abortion because she felt she needed to maintain her independence and her career. She told of the advice her feminist friends had given her and of how they had emphasised her right to organise her life as she saw fit. They had assured her that the feelings experienced by many who had had abortions were simply conditioned by out-of-date social attitudes.

'The feminists think it's OK to have an abortion – that you shouldn't feel anything – that society put this emotional thing on to you. So I was surprised when I did start feeling something. It came from inside me. Now, looking back, the political analysis seems simplistic. I haven't time for that sort of thing. It's self-denying. I realise how deeply affec-ted I am by my biology – much more than I wanted to believe. Your biology makes you much more powerless. I felt how positive it was to be part of something – I felt it in my guts. I felt less lonely when I was pregnant – part of this bigger humanity.

'After the first abortion I was appalled by the hysteria of the other women in the clinic. I was numb, calm, brave, remote. My man arrived when we were having tea, afterwards. There was a great rush of anger from the other women because their men hadn't come. There was a lot of hatred of men, but he busied himself handing round the sandwiches. I was proud of him for being there but we had a fight afterwards. I felt disorientated.'

So, for this woman, the reality was different from the theory. She had not been aware that she was mourning, after her first abortion. But she was quite severely depressed and alienated for many months afterwards. She did not, at first, associate this feeling with the abortion and it was not until after a second abortion, when she was attacked by bouts of uncontrollable weeping that she realised the connection. It seemed to her that to have an abortion, she must be unfeeling. She was confirmed in her worst fears about herself. She was very attracted towards the child of a friend and wanted one of her own.

'I tried to console myself by embracing a pillow. I wanted to hold a child. I was really surprised at this. I felt as if I had had an amputation. It was a physical need. I wanted to talk about it but couldn't. Friends couldn't cope. I was crying all the time. I decided to go to the doctor and he sent me to a counselling group. I felt really emotional, withdrawn, unsure of myself, suspicious of people. I didn't want to know people. I rejected everyone. My illusions were all biting the dust. I wanted to go to London to escape back into the past and its illusions. I knew I couldn't do this. I kept making plans, forgetting that times had changed. I read psychology books trying to make sense of it all, trying to get in touch with the unconscious mind. I felt I was in a void, alone. I felt I couldn't create anything.

'For a time, I needed other people to reflect me. With no reflected image I felt I was nothing. I was living through the image people had of me, but this wasn't really me. The recovery happened in stages. I got this flat and wanted to make a home. There was panic. I wanted to call people, stopped myself, calmed down and felt all right. At first I was completely detached from it all, but now I understand that life is real – I feel closer to the reality of life. I stopped crying. Sometimes, still, I feel very empty.

'A woman said how abortion is like a part of you that dies. Maybe that was what the grief was about. Life is more real now. I can't take it so lightly. You have to stop being a child, yourself.'

## Suicide of a Young Person

Suicide by children, fortunately, is rare, but the figures for suicide in young people – teenagers, especially – have increased steadily over the past 30 years. In America, suicide is now the third commonest cause of death in young men in their late teens and early twenties. This suggests that strong social factors are operating on these young people – factors unlikely to be directly the responsibility of parents. In at least half the cases of adolescent suicide there is clear evidence of psychiatric illness.

Bereavement following suicide is probably worse than any other. On top of all the usual factors the bereaved person almost always suffers a terrible sense of guilt and, in many cases, has to live with the implied or spoken criticism of others. When there is a suicide, most people feel that someone has to be to blame, and society will usually attribute blame to the person closest to the deceased. The result is much worse than just the absence of sympathy – it may be frank accusation. The reaction to this is, understandably, severe, and whether the accusation is accepted or, as is more usual, denied, there is likely to be a serious interference with mourning.

The sense of guilt may be terrible to bear. Suicide, by a loved dependent, seems to imply rejection of parental love, or suggests that that love was not recognised. It suggests that all the previous efforts of the parents, now rendered futile, were considered of no value by the young person. And it blasts all the hopes for the future which had been invested in the child. So there is, inevitably, a dreadful sense that there was no real understanding between the parent and the one who has died, and, with it, the agonizing questions about how such a state of affairs could have come about. Naturally, the older person feels that he or she should have seen some indications of what was happening, and should have been able to do something to prevent it.

If you are the parent of a child who has committed suicide, you will, time and time again, have asked yourself the apparently unanswerable question – why? I can offer you little consolation, but I can offer some possibility of understanding how this tragedy may have happened.

As we have seen, many suicides are not intended to succeed and do so accidentally. Sometimes, after a few sleeping tablets have been taken, there is a stage of disorientation in which the person concerned can go on taking more in an automatic fashion. Deaths by falling, even if staged as suicide attempts, may still be accidental. 'Suicide gestures' by hanging are very dangerous and many of these end in disaster.

Suicide gestures are usually intended to draw the attention of parents or others to the plight of the young person, but tragically, communication between such young people and their parents is often so poor that this is the only way some of them have to express their distress at their sense of their own unimportance. And, tragically, too, parents often have so little insight into the minds of their children that they have no idea of what is going on.

If you feel that this kind of situation was behind the suicide, and wonder whether you are to blame, I would simply say that the causes of failure of communication between the generations are much too complex to be attributed to any one person. Communication failure is related, among other things, to differing attitudes and values. One can only react according to one's own values and opinions, and young people can hardly be expected to share those of a different generation. Young people, today, are the products of very different influences from those of the older generation. These including a vast input of information from television and popular magazines, and much of this influence may be in conflict with the formed values of older people. So, to the age-old classic failure of communication between the generations, has been added a new factor, and of this you are, to some extent, the victim.

# 9 Immediate Practical Matters

Ideally, all those practical matters which can be sorted out beforehand will have been attended to, as part of the preparation for bereavement. But it is unrealistic to expect that this will often happen. The person who has died may have been willing, and anxious, to do as much as possible to help, but, even so, it is still very difficult to suggest that these things should be attended to when to do so implies that death is expected. It can be very difficult indeed for the carer to bring up such matters, and this is so even if serious difficulties are anticipated and there is the risk that important affairs may be left unresolved.

Often the dying person seems indisposed, or may even refuse altogether, to attend to, or even consider, matters of that kind. And, of course, in the case of sudden death, nothing at all may have been done to ease the inevitable burden on the person left behind. Again, however much may have been done beforehand, a death imposes on the person left behind a number of responsibilities which have to be discharged.

So, cruelly, just at the time when you are least able to cope, you are likely to find yourself faced with a heap of practical problems. This is a time at which you are especially vulnerable – a time when you are liable to make mistakes, some of which might have serious consequences. You are largely unprotected and could suffer through not having your usual caution and common sense. You might even become the victim of the unscrupulous – and, regrettably, there are plenty of those about.

If you are fortunate, a good friend will come in and take over. But you may not have such a capable and understanding friend, or it may be that you want to cope yourself, or that some of the matters to be attended to are private to you and not to be disclosed to others.

For all sorts of reasons, you are going to need advice and guidance at this time. I hope that this chapter may help to provide them.

# REGISTRATION OF DEATH

If your loved one has died in hospital you will get quite a lot of help from the hospital authorities. A kind and understanding ward Sister can be a blessing, but she is a very busy person and there is a limit to what she can do. At least she will advise you and will arrange for you to get the death certificate, which will be made out and signed by one of the doctors concerned. The death certificate is an important paper and you must keep it carefully. Should the death be due to an accident, the Sister will inform the police, and, as we shall see in a moment, there are certain circumstances in which the Coroner must be informed. Don't worry about this. It is a routine legal requirement.

If the death occurred at home, the first thing to do is to ring up or contact your family doctor and tell him, or her, that a death has occurred. You need not do this in the middle of the night, and it will be a kindness to a busy doctor to wait until the next morning. If you feel you can't cope, call the doctor. You are not allowed to have the body taken away until it has been seen by a doctor. If you are not the nearest relative, you should inform whoever is, as soon as you reasonably can.

The doctor must confirm the death, and will want to check how things are with you. He or she will also have to make out and give you the death certificate and, if you are living in Britain and can re-member, you should also ask for the National Health Service Medical Card, which the Registrar will want (see below), and which is usually kept by the General Practitioner. In all probability, the doctor will en-quire whether you wany any tablets to help you through your ordeal. Your response is up to you. Help with sleeping, at least for a time, is probably a good idea, but remember that long-term tranquillisers really do no good at all and may even simply postpone your recovery. (See Chapter 7).

If the death was unexpected and the cause not entirely clear, the doctor may not make out a certificate. Try not to be upset if the question of referring the death to the Coroner should come up. This does not necessarily mean that there is any suspicion that something is wrong. It is simply that, for very good reasons there are certain legal requirements which must be met before a certificate can be given. You will find that the Coroner will be involved if death has occurred suddenly for no apparent reason, or if there was anything very unusual, or suspicious about it. He will have to be informed if no doctor had been the deceased during the last illness or within 14 days before or after death, or if the death might have been due to an accident, an assault, neglect, abortion or poisoning.

The death must be registered within five days, and burial or cremation cannot take place until this is done. So once you have the death certificate you, or someone legally entitled to do so, should attend to this. Registration is important to you, as insurance claims, probate (proving) of the will, and other matters cannot be settled without the Registrar's certificates (see below).

Assuming you are a legal 'informant' – that is, one of the list of people who may register a death, you can go ahead. But in the circumstances, you may feel that this is too difficult, and may want someone else to attend to it for you. Fortunately, the doctor will give you a list of qualified informants with the death certificate, and this is quite wide. Registration may be done by the next of kin, or someone nominated as a proxy, or by a relative who was present at the death or during the last illness. If you are not a relative, but were present at the death, or living in the same house, you may register the death.

The death must be registered either in the District where the death occurred or in the District where the deceased normally lived. Either will do. To find out where the Registry office is, look up 'Registration of Births, Deaths and Marriages' in the phone book and check the address for the District concerned. Or you can find out from your doctor, from a Post office, from the Council offices, or from a Public Library. You don't need an appointment. Just go along during business hours. You may have to wait until the Registrar is free to see you.

When you go to see the Registrar you must take the death certificate and the Health Service Medical Card so that the National Health number can be noted. But do remember that the Registrar is going to ask you certain questions about the deceased and you will be spared embarrassment, and perhaps even an extra journey, if you find out or confirm the answers and make a note of them before hand.

Write down the following details about the deceased:

1.  Full names. If a married woman, the maiden name.
2.  Address.
3.  Date of birth.
4.  Place of birth.
5.  Occupation. Full details needed. If a married woman, the occupation of husband.
6.  Details of State pension, or allowances if these were being received at the time of death.

7. Date of death.
8. Place of death.
9. If the deceased was under 16, you will need to provide the full names and occupations of the father and mother.

The Registrar will want to know your particulars, as the 'informant'. When everything is noted and checked, an entry will be made in the register and signed by you. You will be asked to use the Registrar's pen which contains special, non-fading ink.

When all is completed, you can collect from the Registrar various certificates which you may need. If you are not sure what these are, ask him. The disposal certificate, either for burial or cremation, will allow you to go ahead with the funeral, and the standard death certificate will enable you to obtain probate of the will and to make claims on private life insurance policies, pension schemes and Friendly Societies.

But you might need certificates to claim:
1. Widow's benefit.
2. Insurance on the life of a parent or grandparent.
3. Benefits under the Social Security and National Insurance.
4. Claims on National Savings Certificates, National Savings Banks and Premium Bonds.

**The Funeral Director**
It is the job of the funeral director to relieve you of responsibility for attending to the body, and for all the arrangements for, and conduct of, the funeral, including the burial or cremation. This is a service few of us would choose to do for ourselves and you will probably be relieved to have someone to perform it for you. So you should be ready and willing to pay a sum of money to be spared it. The funeral director is likely to be the first person to enter the house after the doctor has certified death. He is an adviser who is likely to know the answers to most of your questions, or those asked by other relatives, he will be suitably sympathetic but not fulsome, helpful, supportive and able to relieve many of your anxieties. You are likely to look on him as a friend.

You are likely to be confused and you may be ignorant of all sorts of details connected with a funeral. The director might, for instance, suggest that the body should be embalmed. This is a preserving process to delay decomposition and involves injecting formalin solution into the blood vessels. Unless there is going to be undue delay before burial this is quite unnecessary and will only add to your expenses. Don't be talked into it, unless you want it. In any case, embalming is illegal until the Registrar's disposal certificate is obtained. Bodies in hospital are refrigerated and embalming is even less necessary in this case.

Most directors, like most people, are reasonably ethical and fair-minded, and few will actually try to cheat you. Many, aware that they are liable to criticism, are scrupulous to avoid taking any unfair advantage of the bereaved. But you should take a realistic view of the matter and remember two things. The funeral director is engaged in a business for profit and, like all business men, aims to make as large a profit as possible. Secondly, the director has a unique psychological advantage over you. Your resistance is low. You may be shocked out of your normal standards of business caution and may even be suffering from a temporary disturbance of judgment so far as matters connected with your loved one are concerned. The experience of the ages has shown that when people have this sort of power over others, there is a strong tendency for it to corrupt. The director is certainly entitled to a fair profit, but he is not entitled to manipulate you ruinously for his advantage.

There has been widespread criticism of the practices of funeral directors in the United States, especially of their deliberate use of applied psychology to persuade grieving relatives to agree to elaborate and expensive funerals, embalming and expensive cosmetic treatment of bodies. Investigation showed that many were inventing non-existent laws for their own ends – laws such as that burial without a casket (coffin) or without embalming were illegal. The pressures on relatives to buy unnecessarily expensive coffins and to take advantage of the buyer's ignorance of the matter, were subtle and powerful. The matter was even looked into by the Federal Trade Commission and recommendations issued. Jessica Mitford's book *The American Way of Death* makes hair-raising reading.

In Britain, the National Association of Funeral Directors, sensitive to the possibility of criticism and wishing their members to be regarded as ethical professionals, have issued a Code of Practice for them. This includes the requirement to be as helpful as possible, to charge fair prices, to give a full estimate of costs on a standard form, to offer, if requested, a simple basic, funeral, and to assist in the investigation of complaints. Even so, the funeral director still has an advantage over you which it is only too easy for him to exploit.

When you visit the funeral parlour or look at catalogues of coffins, be sure you are accompanied by a tough-minded friend.

**Cremation**

Nowadays, about three quarters of all those dying in Britain, West Germany and Denmark are cremated. In India and Japan, the practice is almost universal. In the United States, the proportion is much less – about one tenth only. Interestingly, cremation is a reversion to an ancient practice introduced by the Greeks around 1000 BC. In this historic tradition cremation came to be regarded as the only fitting end for the life of a hero. It is clear from Homer's Iliad how important cremation was considered to be. The Romans took up the Greek tradition and cremation became something of a status symbol. The early Scandinavians also favoured cremation. In India cremation is traditionally regarded as a religious necessity and in Tibet it is used as an honour for the high lamas.

The renewal of interest in cremation in the English-speaking world began in 1874 with the publication of a book on the subject by Sir Henry Thompson and the organisation of the Cremation Society of England. Anthony Trollope, the novelist, was an active member. In 1884 a British court ruled that cremation was legal and soon crematoria were being built, both in England and in the United States. In Europe, shortage of burial space and criticism of the hygienic aspects has led to increased adoption of the practice, and it is now officially accepted by many Protestant churches. Cremation is not prohibited by the Roman Catholic Church, but is unacceptable to those of the orthodox Jewish faith. Reform Jews often chose cremation and have the ashes scattered in a Jewish burial ground.

I mention these facts because I know that many find it a very difficult and emotional problem to decide between cremation and burial. Perhaps some knowledge of the historic context may help you to see cremation in perspective and recognise it as an entirely respectable choice.

Some people are upset by what may seem to be the 'matter-of-factness' of the cremation process. You may find that you are herded a little and you will probably be aware that you are in a line of several funerals. Because of pressure of work, crematoria all work on appointments system and the service must necessarily be short. If you are musically sensitive, be sure to talk to the funeral director about this. You may be one of those who find sentimental taped Hammond Organ musak offensive and may prefer silence, or some real music – like the slow movement of a Mozart or Schubert String Quartet or Quintet.

Your own minister or priest may officiate or one may be provided by the crematorium, on request. You need not have a religious service and can, if you like, have a secular funeral at which a friend, or a member of the family talks briefly about the deceased, perhaps reads something appropriate, leaves a short period of silence for remembrance and then, after the disappearance of the coffin, leads the mourners out of the chapel to the sound of quiet music.

During the cremation service, the coffin passes quietly out of sight of the mourners into a committal room where the name on the coffin is checked against the cremation order (disposal certificate) from the Registrar, and a card with all the needed details is attached to the coffin. The actual cremation takes place as soon as possible after the service and must take place the same day. The card is detached and the coffin is placed in a special incinerator where, in the course of an hour or two, it is transformed by intense heat into a few pounds of powdery ash.

The ashes are put in an urn and you will be asked whether you want to keep them. Don't be hurried about the decision. You may elect to have them scattered in the crematorium garden and you can watch this if you want to. Or you can take them away and scatter them yourself, wherever you like, or perhaps arrange to have them buried in a cemetery. You can keep the urn with the ashes.

There is always provision in crematoria for a memorial of some kind, such as a plaque on a wall, a small area of private ground for scattering the ashes or a book of remembrance. All these things cost money and you are not required to agree to any of them. Remember that the choice is up to you, guided by the known wishes of the deceased. Just be sure that the funeral director clearly understands your wishes.

**Burial**
Burial may take place either in a churchyard or in a cemetery. The churchyard is under church control and the cemetery is controlled by local authorities or private companies. If you live in a parish there is a historic right to be buried in your own parish churchyard. But, today, with the closure of many churches, many parishes have no churchyard and many of those that exist are full. You still have a right to request burial in the churchyard of a neighbouring parish. The decision rests with the vicar and his church council. You will not, however, have the right to select a site for the grave – that is a matter for the vicar. If you have a family grave with space, then there is no problem, so long as the lease has not run out.

People not buried in a churchyard are buried in a cemetery. You can buy the right to a family grave in a cemetery, for a period of so many years – perhaps 50 – and you will be given a deed of grant.

Alternatively, you can buy a common grave or a lawn grave, which are cheaper. Ask your funeral director about this and be sure you are clear about the costs.

Burial involves a number of different fees. These include:
1. The cost of the grave.
2. The cost of digging the grave.
3. The burial fee.
4. The cost of the service.
5. Organist's fee. Choir fee.
6. The cost of heating the church in Winter.
7. The cost of printed sheets for the service.
8. The cost of wreaths and flowers.
9. The cost of the headstone and the inscription.
10. The cost of removing, inscribing and replacing an existing stone.
11. The funeral director's charges.

**Other Things To Attend To**
Remember to notify as many people as possible of the death. Ask those you tell to pass on the news. Remember that it is not just friends and relatives who should be informed. Work associates or professional colleagues should also be notified. You will probably want to put a notice in the local or a national paper. The director will help you with this if you are in doubt. There are several fairly standard forms of wording you may wish to use or you can compose your own notice. If you want people to attend the funeral, you must say where and when it is to be held. And you will have to decide whether you want people to send flowers.

If there is to be a service you may want friends to come back to your house afterwards, or to meet in a hotel or some other convenient place, and you will want to provide some kind of a light meal or buffet. Whether or not you serve drinks will depend on you, but there is something to be said for doing so. Relatives, many of whom may not have seen each other for a long time, and some of whom may have come a long way, will be anxious to have a chance to talk over old times, and drinks can help to reduce constraint. Don't be upset if there is much loud chatter, and even laughter, before long. It is a strange facet of human psychology that the contemplation of the death of one who is not too close, sometimes induces unwanted cheerfulness.

You will, perhaps, wonder what to wear at the funeral. Something quiet, preferably dark, is all that is necessary nowadays. Don't spend money on mourning clothes you are unlikely ever to wear again, unless you particularly want to. You are sure to have something suitable in your wardrobe.

**Settling Financial Affairs**
It is here that foresight and preparation can make the greatest difference. If there is a will, all the sorting out of the financial affairs is the responsibility of the executor nominated in it. If there is no will, you, as the closest relative, or the surviving spouse, are going to have to sort out the estate yourself. The best advice is to seek professional advice. Matters are *never* as simple as they seem, and this is no job for the amateur or armchair lawyer. You will almost certainly need help and advice and you would do very well to consult a solicitor. This doesn't commit you to having the solicitor take on the whole business of managing the estate, and you can work out at the first interview whether you merely want advice or the full service.

If there is no will and you are the surviving spouse and there are no other relatives, everything the deceased had will pass to you after settlement of death duties. If there are children or other relatives, you still get all your spouse's personal 'chattels' – things like furniture, jewellery, cars, pictures, ornaments, wines, and so on. But the rules include provision for the children and the others. The balance is always greatly in favour of the surviving spouse. Your solicitor will explain everything.

If there is a will, the executor's job is to get the will officially agreed – that is, to obtain Grant of Probate – to collect together all the assets, pay all outstanding debts, including the funeral expenses, solicitor's fees, and inheritance taxes, and distribute the balance in accordance with the terms of the will.

If there is no will, much the same things happen, but someone has to become the administrator of the estate. This is likely to be you, and your action will depend on how much is left – the size of the estate. To estimate this, you ignore the value of the jointly owned house, ignore any money in joint accounts or the value of jointly held stocks or shares, and see what is left. If the whole total remaining is less than about £5,000 you will probably be able to go ahead and obtain the assets simply by producing the death certificate. But if the estate is larger than this, see a solicitor. The matter becomes more complicated and the question of who should administer the estate may arise.

The rules are that application for grant of Letters of Administration – to make the business official – should normally be made by the next of kin of the deceased. The next of kin must be a person over the age of 17, and the identity is decided according to the following priority:

Surviving spouse

Son or daughter

Father or mother

Brother or sister

Other relatives

If you are to be the administrator, the following is a very broad outline of what you will have to do:

1. You will have to apply to the local Probate Office for forms to obtain Letters of Administration – the equivalent of Grant of Probate. You will be given forms to take away and complete. On these you will have to enter the full personal details of the deceased and yourself.
2. You will have to find out everything that was owned by the deceased, including private (not joint) bank, current and deposit account, balances; building society balances; unit trusts; national savings certificates; stocks and shares; premium bonds; cash; personal property and household goods (valued at the date of death); and business assets. Shares must be valued at the current 'bid' price.
3. You must find out about any money owed to the deceased and about any outstanding pay or salary due from an employer.
4. You must check all insurance policies and note the beneficiary.
5. You will have to find out everything that is owed by the deceased, including mortgage; rates; water rates; rent; service charges; gas; electricity and telephone accounts; hire purchase; loans; credit card balances and outstanding income tax.
6. You may have reason to suspect that there are other creditors (people to whom money is owed) and you can advertise, using a standard wording, asking them to make claims within two months.
7. You will have to enter all these particulars in the forms and take or send them back, with the death certificate, to the Probate Office.
8. You will then have to visit the Probate Office again to obtain the grant of Letters of Administration.
9. You can then distribute the estate.

Note that no one is liable for other people's debts. If, for instance, your husband died leaving unpaid bills, and without enough money in the estate to pay, you are not required to pay them from your own money.

## The House

You may be worrying about your entitlement to your house. If the house was in both your names, and declared, at the time of purchase, or later to be 'held on trust for themselves as joint tenants beneficially', then you become the owner of the whole interest in the house. The solicitor who did the conveyancing will tell you the terms of the agreement. If some other form of words was used, such as, 'held by the parties in equal shares', you will not *automatically* inherit the deceased's share. The share may have been left to someone else. If there is no will, complications may arise and the outcome will depend on the existence of other relatives. See your solicitor.

You may be in a rented house or flat. If you are a widow, the tenancy automatically passes from the deceased to you. The same applies if you were not married but living together openly as man and wife. Otherwise the tenancy passes to any other member of the deceased's family who was living with him at his death and for the six months prior to death.

**Investment**
You are likely to be worried about this. It may be that you are now in possession of more money than you have ever had in your life and it is possible that you have very little idea how to lay it out to the best and most secure advantage. Right now, your responsibility is to do *nothing*.

See that the money is in a high interest bank deposit account or in a building society, and do nothing. There will be plenty of people only too ready to advise you – people who will tell you that you are throwing away money by not having it in a unit trust, or in gilts, or in gold. Ignore them. Just remember what happened to the Stock Market in October, 1987. Read the next chapter carefully. Get sound, independent advice. Insist on having security and a conservative investment, rather than the possibility of high profits. Peace of mind is much more important than a few thousand extra in your portfolio. Wait until you are sure you are able to make a sound choice before signing away a penny.

# 10 Widowhood

Even in this age of sexual equality, a woman's status is still very often tied to that of her husband. This is especially so of the elderly woman. Perhaps you have found this – that people treat you differently from before, show less respect, make you feel unimportant. I expect you are also aware that, however self-reliant you may try to be, as a woman without a husband, you are more liable to fall victim to those who prey on the defenceless. Under the veneer of civilisation the world is still a jungle where creatures prey on one another and where the solitary must look out more sharply than ever before. I am not referring so much to physical danger – although this is now very real – as to the dangers to your finances and to your civil rights.

As a widow, you must look to every means of protecting yourself. You must find out, and take advantage of, every existing right. You need knowledge and, if possible, advice and protection. You should try, if you can, to get allies – friends, supportive companions, possibly even a new husband. You should consider how far you can establish a new status of your own.

You may consider this an impossible task, especially late in life, but as we shall see in Chapter 12, you are going to change, whatever happens, and the only question is – what sort of a person will you be? Here is a story which brings out a number of important points.

### A Chance of Life
Jean Partington's husband died when she was fifty-seven and it was not long before she discovered that she had lost more than simply companionship, support and love. She was an intelligent, attractive woman, who would have liked to fend for herself, but Francis had been the tougher-minded of the two, a man who had taken all the decisions and always put himself forward. He had been the one in charge, and it was his personality that had always been impressed on others with whom they had dealings. He had

been a highly successful manager of a firm making electric light fittings.

Jean found that now she had to manage on her own, she was much less capable then she had expected. This was mainly because of her lack of experience in dealing with people. After Francis's death she soon found a notable difference in the attitude of most people who came to the house. She was treated with less politeness and little deference. She was even subjected to some mild sexual harassment. A plumber who came in to fix the ball-cock in the upstairs loo, and to whom she offered a friendly cup of coffee, made unequivocal suggestions that they might retire to the bedroom. When she had managed to get rid of him, and had noted that the bill was considerably larger than the estimate, she vowed, even at her age, to learn at least some elementary household do-it-yourself.

They had had no children and, although she owned the house and had some income from Francis's investments, she was far from affluent, and it occurred to her that taking a job might help on more than one count. Eventually, after a number of disappointments and progressive lowering of sights, she was able to get employment, nominally as a filing and accounts clerk, but actually as a very useful secretary and general dogsbody, to a firm of wholesale purveyors of household equipment. The pay, unfortunately, was that of a filing clerk and, although she soon came to realise that she was being exploited, felt herself in no position to complain.

Her working companions were, in general, pleasant, and she soon became 'auntie' to the younger members and established friendly relationships with most of the staff. Coming to the firm with an open mind, she soon began to suspect that the business methods used were inefficient, rigid and wasteful. Many activities appeared to be performed for no better reason than that 'they had always been done that way.' The accounting was so cumbersome and obscure that she could see opportunities for almost undetectable fraud. When her questions failed to elicit reasons for the methods of organisation, it quickly became apparent to her that no one had a proper grip on the firm. Even so, it seemed profitable and was regularly taking on more staff.

The owner, and Managing Director, of the firm, George, had been a partner with his older brother, who had sold out to him so that he could spend his declining years in his garden. Kenneth had been the prime mover in the firm and had got things going. Since Kenneth's retirement, George, who was now in his early sixties, had been coasting. He was comfortable, easy-going man who left most of the running of the firm to the manager – Jean's immediate boss – but who came in every day to sit in his office and think about fishing.

Meantime, her interest having been aroused, Jean began looking into her personal finances. Attracted by an advertisement in a Sunday paper, she sent off her name and address to a firm of 'Investment Consultants' who held out golden promises of increased income *and* capital gains. Within a day or two she was telephoned by a charming-sounding young man with a cultivated accent and a soothing and reassuring manner who asked a few general questions, indicated that her affairs were too complex to discuss over the telephone, and suggested that he pay her a visit.

The young man was indeed charming, and the interview was pleasant and reassuring. Although Jean did not completely follow everything he told her, she found the evidence he presented of the past successes of schemes, similar to what he was proposing, impressive and exciting. This was prior to the Stock Market crash of October 1987. She had been generally aware that the equity on the house had been rising steadily, but she had not known that she could cash in on this to raise capital, and still stay in the house. The young man gently urged her to do so, pointing out that money tied up in the property was not 'working for her.' The amount offered amazed her.

The income from Francis's portfolio had been enough to meet her day-to-day expenses, rates, and household bills, but the young man held out the promise of much better things, if she would agree to letting his firm dispose of the stocks and shares and put the money into a managed fund. The managers of this, he said, would watch the market closely, regularly adjusting their holdings to maximum benefit, disposing of poor performance stock and investing in companies likely to do well. Income would be credited monthly to her bank account . . .

So Jean signed a few documents, wrote a few cheques, received some impressive-looking certificates and congratulated herself on her financial acumen.

The first sign of trouble came one morning, about three months later, when a letter arrived containing a cheque and a bank slip marked 'refer to drawer.'

The upshot, eventually clarified with the assistance of a solicitor, on the 'Green form' scheme, was that the firm she had trusted with her money had been established only a little over a year before, that the men running it were inexperienced and had over-reached themselves.

Jean was now in an extremely difficult situation with only the income from her job to meet the rates, the gas, electricity, telephone, clothes and food. She was overdrawn at the bank and had some credit card debts. So she sold her car and bought a Yamaha motor scooter with an electric starter and an automatic gear-box. She was nervous, but desperate, and was lucky enough to have no trouble in the early stages and soon acquired confidence. To her surprise, she found she could now get to work more quickly than when she was driving her car.

She was at the stage of considering having her telephone taken out when George asked if she would consider having him as a lodger.

'It's a fine big house, you have,' he said, 'near the river and handy for the job. I'm getting fed up with coming all the way down from Bishop's Stortford and I've had an amazing offer for my house. What do you say?'

'I never considered . . .'

'I wouldn't be a bother. I just need a room, maybe two. I'm a tidy chap. Maybe if you could just get me a bite of breakfast – oh, and some little thing for supper . . . You know . . .'

Jean hastily refrained from pointing out that she was working all day and said she would think about it.

George offered to pay a generous rent, and, in the end, driven by necessity, and the awareness that his provided a solution to her immediate problem, Jean agreed. The outcome was happier than she had expected. Having been accustomed for years to having a man in the house, it was a positive relief to have the company and to know that there was someone close to whom she could turn in emergency.

At the same time she was realistically suspicious of his motives and assumed that he would expect more for his money than had nominally been agreed. In this she was mistaken. George's behaviour was impeccable and he was the ideal tenant, quiet, courteous and considerate, keeping himself to himself except when she encouraged him to talk, but friendly and helpful, in a detached sort of way. Soon after he moved in he remarked that it was ridiculous for them to go separately to work, he in his car and she on her scooter, and so they went together – a circumstance the staff did not fail to notice. He had two rooms, a bedroom and sitting room, and at first he had his meals alone. But within a month she felt secure enough to suggest that it would be less trouble if he took his meals with her.

'Are you sure you want that?' he asked, 'I don't want to intrude on you.'

'You wouldn't. There's no need to talk, unless you want to.'

But talk was what they did – endlessly. By now, Jean was beginning to formulate some ideas of her own about how the business should be run, and, very diplomatically, she began to put these to him. She had made an analysis, in the form of a sort of flow-chart, of everything that happened in the business, and of the activities of each member of the staff. She had then drawn another chart to show what had to be done. A comparison of the two highlighted the fact that about a quarter of the staff time was taken up with unproductive and futile activity.

George looked at her charts, made a few minor comments and said, 'OK. We'll try it your way. But I won't have anyone dismissed.'

'Then we'll have to expand.'

'Why not? We're turning away business right now.'

'Exactly. Just what I hoped you would say.'

Jean's enthusiasm seem to awaken in him a renewed interest in the business and soon they were spending most evenings together going over their developing plans. At first, when business talk languished he would make a move to excuse himself and go up to his rooms, but often Jean would suggest that he stay and have a night-cap. On these occasions, the talk ranged widely and Jean soon found that he was a much more interesting man than she had supposed.

One evening he told her something about his earlier life. He had been a successful rubber planter in Malaya, but had left after his estate had been attacked by Chinese communist terrorists during the Emergency and most of his people hacked to death. Much to her surprise, she found that he had had a Malay wife – a beautiful girl who had died in saving him from murder. He had never before mentioned her, and had been assumed to be a bachelor.

'Were you very much in love?'

'We were. It only lasted two years. She was the loveliest thing you ever saw. Her skin was marvellous and she walked like a princess. She made me feel like ...'

'Like a king?'

'Yes.'

'So you never married again?'

'I could never find anyone who came near to her. I suppose, in the end, I stopped looking.'

They were silent for a long time, and then looked at each other.

'You miss your man?' he asked.

'Oh yes, desperately ...' Then, without thinking, she added, 'But you help, a lot.'

As he left to go up, that evening, George laid his hand, for a moment, on her shoulder.

Within six months, Jean was managing the import side of the business and two years later they were married.

Taking a job is something you should always consider seriously, whatever your circumstances. Work can be a solace, a new interest in life, a source of needed income or of jam on the butter. It is an excellent way to meet new people, to make friends and, perhaps, even to find a second husband. Taking a tenant will not always work out as satisfactorily as it did for Jean, but it is something you ought to consider, if practicable.

## Remarriage and Sex

Remarriage is unlikely, at first, to seem an attractive option, but you need not feel guilty, or think that there is something wrong with you if the matter is often in your thoughts. Studies have shown that a high proportion of widows seriously desire remarriage. Of course, you should certainly be very hesitant, and extremely selective, before even considering it. But experience shows that second marriages are frequently happier than the first.

And now that you are older and, I trust, wiser, you are better qualified to assess people and not to be taken in by superficial attractions. You will, or ought to have learned by now that qualities like honesty, fair-mindedness, generosity, understanding, tolerance and kindness are far more important than good looks, or the ability to dress well, or to be up with the latest modes in speech and opinion. Shared interests and goals, companionship and a reasonably common outlook on life are the essential ingredients.

The loss of a husband involves, in addition to everything else, the loss of a sexual partner. You may have reached the menopause, and you may have discovered that the prevalent idea that this spells the end of a woman's sexual interest in nonsense. Everyone is different, but for most women it is a relief from the anxiety over the possibility of pregnancy and a welcome beginning to a life of care-free sexual satisfaction. For a widow, who had reached this stage, the loss of the partner may be a sore deprivation.

There is plenty of evidence that many widows, who had been happily married, suffer a deep sense of sexual deprivation. Many of them also feel deeply guilty at having such thoughts. The worst hit are those whose previous experience of sex was very good, and in these cases it would be as unreasonable to criticise such longings as to object to the longing for companionship. An acute sense of sexual deprivation may be experienced very soon after the death – perhaps even the first time the widow sleeps alone – and for some highly sexed people this may be the foremost concern. Such a situation is a recipe for powerful guilt feelings, especially if, as happens more often than one would imagine, the strength of the sexual desire precipitates the act, soon after the death, with some friend, casual acquaintance or even a stranger.

If this has happened to you, take such comfort as you can in the knowledge that it has happened many times and that it happens because sex occurs for hormonal and psychological reasons which are often much stronger than either our reason or our will.

Many widows are tempted into casual affairs, but these are likely to be sadly unfulfilling. Many mature people, like Jean, do not regard sex as an end in itself, but only as an expression of love and affection in a serious relationship. For the purely physical tensions of sex – and these can be strong and troublesome – masturbation is to be preferred either to casual sex or to stressful, long-sustained, repression. It is a natural act, unfortunately associated in the minds of many of us with ideas of sinfulness. These were induced in childhood at a time when anything linked with such an emotive subject inevitably produced a powerful and permanent effect. But if these primitive responses can be ignored, self-induced orgasm can be helpful to the solitary. You will *not* form permanent habits – unless you are so unfortunate as to remain permanently without a partner. And as soon as you do establish a proper sexual relationship, masturbation will be forgotten.

There is one very important point in connection with forming serious new relationships. We have seen that the mourning process must be worked through and that this takes time. If you establish a close relationship with another man soon after your bereavement, it is likely that you are merely using him as a substitute for your lost husband. This is no basis for a future relationship, so give yourself time.

## Money

You can learn a lot, too, from Jean's financial disaster. There are plenty of cold-hearted, money-worshipping people around who will gladly deprive you of your vital little nest-egg if you will let them. There are also plenty of people who genuinely believe they can make money for you, while creaming off a nice percentage for themselves, but who are, in fact, minnows in the shark-infested waters of speculative finance, and may gamble with your money and lose. Watch out, too, for the sharks who look you candidly in the eye, grasp you by the hand and ask you, 'Do you sincerely want to be rich?' Of one thing you can be completely certain – whatever they say, these people are not in it for your benefit. The only philanthropists in the money world are those who have already made their pile and now want to try to buy some public respect.

It may be that, as a recent widow, you are, for the first time in your life, in possession of a substantial sum of money. Inheritances or insurance money often come in alarmingly large lumps and you may not have had previous experience of handling more than a small personal account. If you are in this situation you are vulnerable. You may feel that the sheer size of the sum means that you need no longer be careful. Watch out!

You will start looking at the financial pages of the Sunday papers and doing little calculations of how much interest you may be earning or how much capital growth you might be enjoying. If you reply to an advertisement, you are likely to find someone on your doorstep, or on the telephone, who will not easily be put off. An attitude of sustained scepticism is always safest. *Never* make a major investment without taking independent advice. Speak to your bank manager or solicitor or a knowledgable friend.

Anyone trying to persuade you to go into a scheme should be told frankly that you propose to take advice. If the matter is above board there will be no objection. If there is objection, drop the proposal at once. The psychology of the hard sell has been carefully worked out and many salespersons are very good at making you feel that it is unworthy of you, or even insulting, not to trust them. This is all part of the technique. Don't fall for it. If you are being badgered on the telephone, just put down the receiver.

Don't pay too much attention to graphs illustrating fund growth. The fund in question may appear to have been beaten, not only inflation and the building societies, but also the Financial Times 100 share index. But this tells you only how it has done in the past, and gives no information whatsoever about how it will perform in the future. Remember how quickly all the graphs disappeared from the advertisements after the stock market crash of October, 1987.

Every 'investment' is a gamble and you must decide the degree of risk. It is a very fair rule that the higher the return promised, the greater the likelihood of loss. You can assume that the risk is proportional to the interest rates offered and that is why, in general, Government bonds and National Savings offer conservative rates.

Note that building societies, banks and other sources of interest automatically deduct tax at a little below the basic rate before paying interest. This is fine if you are paying tax, but disastrous if you are not, as you will not be able to reclaim the tax deducted. If your income is too low to attract tax,you must not consider leaving money in a bank deposit account or a building society. Go for Government or other income bonds paying interest at the gross rate.

On the other hand, if you have inherited a fair sum, you could be losing a lot of money by leaving it in a bank deposit account or a building society, especially if you pay tax at a rate higher than the minimum. At this point, tax becomes the central consideration and you must look at tax-saving alternatives. You are not entitled to evade tax but you have a legal right to avoid paying any more than is due, and plenty of people are doing that. There are many factors to be considered in the light of your own particular needs and you will certainly require independent advice – if you can get it. Don't resent having to pay for it. Good advice will save you much more than the cost of it. Just try to be sure that your adviser is not simply an agent for an insurance company or a unit trust.

**An Investment Portfolio**
The first and most important thing is to be clear in your mind about what you need from investments. You must work out how much income you require – and this may be more than you think. You need to know whether you need to have cash readily available, and how much. Money tied up in shares or unit trusts is expensive to release in the short term and you will certainly lose money if you have to sell soon after you have bought. You will lose the difference between the 'offer' price, at which you bought, and the 'bid' price, which is what you will get for them. In addition, in the short term, shares and units may well have fallen.

You must decide whether your life is going to be ruined by worry over the risk of investment, or whether you can comfortably live with the knowledge that your fortune is fluctuating with every breath that blows from Wall Street. You have to decide whether you are primarily interested in capital growth or in income and whether that decision is a permanent or a temporary one. You have to consider insurance and any financial responsibility you may have, or wish to undertake, for others. You must get interested in the rate of inflation and consider what would happen if it were to change markedly either way. You may wish to try to cover yourself against both eventualities by putting some of your money into index-linked gilts or index-linked National Savings.

You may even find that you are becoming fascinated by gilts. Just remember that, although they are backed by the British Government, you can still lose a lot of money, especially if you have to dispose of your holding before maturity. Keep out of gilts if you think interest rates are going to rise. If you are paying little tax, buy high interest gilts, and if you are paying a lot of tax, go for low coupon gilts.

**Annuities**
If you are elderly, an annuity might be a good proposition for you. This means that you hand over a lump sum to an insurance company and they pay you a guaranteed income for the rest of your life. The company is gambling on your dying soon, so if you outwit them and live to be a hundred and ten, you will have done very well out of your annuity. If you die soon, you won't be worried. So an annuity is a good bet unless you particularly want to leave money to a relative or friend.

The older you are when you buy the annuity, the higher the income you get. One advantage of an annuity is that much of your income will be tax free. This is because some of it is treated as if it were a return to you of part of your capital. But watch out for the effects of inflation on a fixed income. Annuities are a 'best buy' at a time when interest rates are high, because, if bought then, the income agreed upon will be higher, and will not be affected by a subsequent drop in interest rate.

You should start by finding out what kinds of annuities are available and which kind will suit you best, bearing in mind that the income, for a given lump sum, varies both with the type of annuity and with the company. So you should shop around. Different companies offer quite different terms and there are at least a hundred of them in Britain.

**Home Income Plans**
If you own your house, you can consider a home income plan. This can be done in several ways. You can sell your house at full current market value, but retain a legal right to stay in it until you die, by paying a nominal rent of £1 per month. You then buy an annuity with the money. But remember that you will have no advantage from any further increase in the value of the house, and, of course, you can't leave it to anyone, because it no longer belongs to you. Another way is to borrow part of the value of the house from an insurance company, securing the loan by a mortgage. With the money borrowed you buy an annuity and part of this is used to pay the interest on the mortgage. The remainder is income. This way, you don't lose your title to the house.

There are other ways of cashing in on the value of your house, which may be more suitable for you. But do be ab- solutely clear in your mind about the effects of what you are doing. If you have a house, you have a very considerable, and growing, asset. Other people may be even more aware of this than you are.

### Taking a Lodger

If you are living alone in a reasonably large house you should at least consider the possibility of having a tenant. In many urban areas, the rise in the price of houses and flats has produced a strong demand for letted accommodation, and there are many young people desperate for somewhere to live which is reasonably near their place of work. Quite apart from the advantage to yourself, in additional income and, perhaps, company, you could be doing someone else a great favour. The Department of the Environment has produced a leaflet about letting rooms in your home and you can get this from a D. of E. office or a Citizens Advice Bureau.

Be sure you are familiar with the current regulations on tenancy and don't rush into becoming a landlady. Try to decide the kind of tenant you want. Tell your friends so that, if possible, you get a tenant personally recommended by someone you trust. Failing that, go to a letting agency and tell them exactly what you want. Be cautious. In general, a widow will be better off with a young girl as a tenant, but there are obvious advantages in having a man. You are perfectly entitled to interview and to reject possible tenants and you don't have to give a reason, but you may save yourself embarrassment if you already know the prospective lodger. An interview is best conducted in the presence of a friend. It need not be formal – just a little chat over a cup of coffee to find out about the prospect and to see whether you think he or she might suit.

If you do take a tenant, don't load up the letted room or rooms with all your most valuable antique furniture. You must give your tenant the freedom to arrange the rooms as he or she sees fit. Tenants will probably have things of their own and may need minimal furniture. Whatever you leave in the rooms is going to wear and perhaps be damaged, and you should accept this as part of the deal. You may even wish to refurnish the rooms with plain, new or used, items so that you will be spared the upset of seeing your cherished possessions deteriorate.

In general, you must consider the letted rooms no longer yours. Your tenant is paying for, and will expect, absolute privacy and you must never trespass unless invited. You are not even entitled to assume that your tenant will want to spend the time of day chatting. Many tenants will, of course, and often a very friendly and supportive relationship develops, but that is a bonus and not part of the deal.

## House Maintenance

If you are not a very 'practical' person, one thing that will worry you is how to cope with the many little jobs about the house that your husband used to do. Things like changing electric plugs, replacing fuses, changing tap washers, coping with broken windows, minor painting jobs, and so on.

You can view this in two ways. Either you wring your hands and assume that every such job must either be done by someone else or not at all; or you take my word for it that most of these small domestic jobs are easy and that, given a little know-how and one or two simple tools, can be done by anyone. You only have to change a plug once, and you have got it. It is simply a matter of doing things in the right order.

To get in a man to do such a job is expensive. Nowadays, electricians and plumbers charge a 'call-out' fee which will, itself, greatly exceed the value of the work done, so you should have nothing to do with them unless the job is big enough to justify this. Get a well-illustrated Do-it-Yourself book or ask a handy friend to show you. Better still, do both. Your friend might learn something.

Some of the more ambitious tasks – things like coping with burst pipes – are likely to be beyond you. And you must always remember the danger of domestic accidents happening to elderly people unaccustomed to such work. Try to find out whether there are any *retired* people in the neighbourhood with an interest in household tasks of this kind. It is becoming common for useful skills of this kind, which would gladly be exercise, to be wasted simply for want of communication.

From where I sit at my word processor I can see, down the hill, the immaculate house-front of the eighty-one year old widower, Percy Bligh, the neighbourhood handiman, who will tackle anything from putting up shelves to painting the whole exterior of a house. Percy works slowly, but thoroughly and is a God-send to many. He says he would rather work for nothing than remain idle. Try to find a Percy if you can. You might be doing him a favour.

Make sure that your security arrangements are satisfactory. Proper locks on all the windows and strong mortice locks on the doors are a minimal requirement. Most burglaries are by invitation. Mark the items most likely to be stolen – things like television, sets, video tape recorders, Hi-Fi, cameras – with your postal code, using an indelible felt tip marking pen. This is as good as a name and address and is a great deterrent to burglars.

Major items of maintenance involving structural alteration or re-placement can be very expensive indeed and you should always look into the possibility that you may be entitled to a local council grant for such purposes. All local councils have various schemes for helping owner-occupiers to maintain their property. If your house is more than about 70 years old and needs damp-proofing or roof maintenance, if there is no fixed bath, or a hot water supply, if there is no loft insulation or hot water tank insulation, you may be entitled to a grant. You can even, sometimes, get a grant of money for home improvement such as a kitchen extension or new electric wiring. At present, different councils have different rules so you will have to check with your own council whether you are entitled. One thing is certain – you won't get it if you don't ask.

# 11 The Importance of Health

You may have heard stories about death rates being higher among bereaved people than others of the same age. Well, I have had a close look at the professional papers on this and it is clear that the statistics do not necessarily indicate that it is the death of the spouse that cause the higher risk. One has to be very careful about statistics. What the researchers have done is to lump together all the cases of death following bereavement and, sure enough, the death rate is higher than in people of who not been bereaved. But if you remember that couples share the same, possibly unfavourable, environment, or tend to have the same unhealthy habits, or even suffer the same diseases, then you will see that the reduced life expectancy of the survivor need have nothing to do with being bereaved.

The figures show that men often do badly, especially in the first six months, and that the mortality in that group is quite a lot higher than in a comparable married group of the same age. In this case, there are several possible explanations. Many such men been accustomed to being well looked after by their wives and some simply don't know how to look after themselves. In addition, it is clear that women often do keep men's bad habits in check and that widowers tend to 'go to the dogs'. Many widowers fail to feed themselves properly and smoke and drink far more than is good for them. Cirrhosis of the liver and lung cancer are common causes of death in such men.

At least one study of over 500 bereaved people showed that, for women, bereavement seemed actually to be protective. There was no significant increase in the chance of dying during the first six months and the life expectancy appeared to be slightly increased at about two years after the death of the husband. Other studies, and they are in the majority, show that the risks for widows are slightly greater at about two years, but that this increased risk soon passes off.

So I think we can dismiss, as alarmist, the suggestions that the bereaved are seriously at risk of an early death. Nevertheless it is extremely important to take an intelligent interest in the special health factors affecting bereaved people. Let us look first at the question of stress.

## Stress

Much of what is written about this is simplified and exaggerated and you should not be too strongly influenced by what you read. In Chapter 6 is an account by a sensitive and intelligent woman, still mourning the death of her mother, who is haunted by the fear that her stress reactions to her mother's death must have so damaged her immune system that she, too, was sure to develop breast cancer. This woman had read some popular accounts of the relationship of stress to immunology and had at once jumped to this conclusion.

Stress is an essential and normal part of life and we are all experiencing it, to some degree, all the time. Worrying, suffering embarrassment, having new experiences, mastering a difficult task, watching horror films, having a sense of social inferiority, sitting examinations, taking exercise, suffering pain, fright, cold, shock, infection – the list is endless – are all stress-producing events, and all of us have been experiencing these, and many more, all our lives. To cope with these many small and large demands, our bodies at once respond, to an appropriate degree, by the production of a number of hormones – powerful chemical substances that flow into the blood and are carried to every part of the body. The most important of these are cortisol and adrenaline. We have already touched on the effects of adrenaline; cortisol, like adrenaline, is produced by a pair of small glands sitting on top of the kidneys, known as the adrenals.

Nowadays, physiologists define 'stress' as any event which causes an increased output of cortisol. Cortisol, also known as hydro-cortisone, is a natural steroid ('sterol-like') substance, essential for health and normal living and without it we would die. The substance was synthesised in 1950 and became available to doctors for medical use, as a most valuable, and often life-saving, drug. One of its actions in the body is to release protein from the muscles and to stimulate its conversion into the fuel, glucose, which is essential for coping with the stress. This action is the reason why children exposed to severe stress, or children given steroids, may fail to grow properly. Another action of cortisol is to tighten up arteries so as to prevent a dangerous fall in blood-pressure.

When cortisone is given in very high dosage it has a powerful effect in reducing inflammation and this is often medically valuable – as in allergy, arthritis and other diseases. But inflammation has to do with the body's resistance to infection and that is closely connected with the immune system. Cortisol, in large amounts, prevents vessels from dilating and so bringing essential blood to a part of the body in need; it reduces the ease with which important white cells called phagocytes can get to an area where they can combat infecting organisms; it interferes with the action of lymphocytes ('B' cells and 'T' cells) so that antibody production is reduced and lymphocyte control of virus infection, and even of cancer, may be prejudiced.

Large doses may also accelerate the development of high blood pressure, interfere with the normal menstrual cycle, promote stomach ulcers and, most seriously of all, may hasten the development of atherosclerosis – the 'furring-up' disease of arteries which leads to coronary thrombosis, stroke, and other catastrophes. Atherosclerosis is the number one killer in the western world, accounting for well over half of all deaths.

What we simply do not yet know for certain is whether long-persistent 'natural' rises in cortisol can have the same effect. The probability is that, to an extent varying with the individual, they do. We know that different people produce different levels of cortisol for apparently the same stress, and that these differences tie in with characteristic personality types. We also know that people with 'stressful' personalities do have a greater tendency to develop those diseases which excess cortisol can lead to.

But one must keep a sense of proportion and appreciate that the data on these matters is statistical and can be misleading. There seems to be little doubt that prolonged high levels of stress are undesirable, but it is also clear that there are plenty of people who thrive on them. A bereavement is certainly one of the major stress events of life – the degree of stress depending on the degree of dependence and loss, and if you have reason to suppose that high stress levels are continuing, you should certainly watch out for, and report, the earliest signs of illness.

There is good reason to believe that effective relaxation can lower stress of all kind. The inter-relationship of the mind and the body is so close that everything that affects one, affects the other. An unhappy state of mind will, as we have seen, produce tensions and other bodily reactions which are damaging. But it is also true that if you can somehow succeed in releasing these tensions, you may be able to induce a measure of serenity of mind. Perhaps you are smiling wryly and asking how someone in your position can possibly relax, but this merely points the moral that stress-induced tension requires training for its release.

So try on your own, by all means, but you are likely to find that you will need the help of a trained person, such as a physiotherapist or an occupational therapist. If you live in a town, you will almost certainly find that evening classes in relaxation are available. So add these to the list of worth-while activities which I hope you will be compiling before you have finished reading this book.

## Nutrition

Most of us eat too much, and the temporary reduction in food intake which commonly accompanies the sadness and depression of bereavement is unlikely to do much harm to those who are normally a little overweight. But for some, and especially those whose normal appetite is small, any reduction can be dangerous. If you don't eat, your body still needs fuel to keep going. First it uses up all the fat stored under your skin and elsewhere, converting it into glucose which the body burns up for energy. When the fat is all consumed – and this will not take very long if you are naturally thin – your muscles are called on to supply the vital fuel and these soon waste away. This is very serious as it leads to weakness and disability and you will find it very difficult to put the bulk back into the wasted muscles.

So anorexia (persistent loss of appetite) is especially dangerous in the elderly whose muscles are already weakened and wasted by disuse.

Some bereaved people take so little interest in food that, although they do eat, they subsist on a fixed and insufficiently varied diet – perhaps just buns and tea. This kind of a diet will provide calories but will be so short of vitamins that sooner or later you will begin to suffer from vitamin deficiency diseases. It is hard to believe that elderly people living in the midst of our affluent society can suffer from scurvy – the vitamin C deficiency disease which used to affect sailors on long sea voyages whose diet consisted only of sea biscuits and salted pork – but it is so. Bleeding from the gums, massive bruising, severe arthritis from bleeding into the joints, and other unpleasant effects, can occur after about three months on a diet limited to tea and muffins.

It is easy to get enough vitamins, and any diet, however meagre, which contains a little fruit and fresh vegetables, some milk, fish and cheese, and an occasional chicken leg or some minced beef, will give you all you need. You may be in despair and think that there is no point in bothering, but your grief will pass and if, in the meantime you have done yourself an injury by malnutrition, the effects may still be there to add to your difficulties at a time when you have problems enough trying to rebuild your life.

## Exercise

Health is activity, and although, at present, you may feel that the last thing you want to do is to be active, I assure you that this is one of the best remedies for your present unhappiness. The body is amazingly responsive, even in old age, and will, given time, adapt so as to be able to perform much of what you ask it to do. This was well brought out by a trial carried out on over 100 people in their seventies and eighties in California. These people were started on gentle exercising, well within their capacity, walking, jogging, swimming, stretching and performing yoga. Many could hardly walk when they started but, with careful progression of the exertion, excellent results, in terms of improved physical ability, were obtained. Many men were able, within six months, to jog for a mile without stopping. The lung air capacity increased by about 20 per cent and the amount breathed in a given time rose by as much as 35 per cent.

This was an important study in that it brought out the fact that one is *never* too old to enjoy an improvement in physical capacity by trying. But the adaptability of the body works in the opposite direction also. We now know that too much rest is dangerous. Enforced bed rest, as a result of illness, leads to loss of power which may take much longer to recover from than the length of the period spent in bed. For this reason, all enlightened doctors now minimise bed rest, and get patients moving as soon as possible. I have dealt with this question in some detail in another book *(Stroke!* David & Charles, Publishers, 1987).

You should aim to take a reasonably long walk at least twice a week. The more often, the better; the longer the better; the brisker the better. If you can walk up a hill and down the other side, do so rather than going round on the flat. Regular physical exercise is as good for the mind as it is for the body. It induces a sense of optimism, relieves depression, encourages constructive thought, and prompts the imagination. Wordsworth used to walk for hours composing poetry in his mind. Then he would go home and write it all down.

Try to provide yourself with a good motive for walking, a dog, for instance.

## Pets

If you are living alone, do consider the the advantages of keeping a pet. Pets, such as dogs or cats, provide company, comfort, sometimes protection, and may have a major role in promoting social intercourse. Dog owners who take regular walks tend to meet others engaged in the same activity or working in gardens. One cannot pass the same person repeatedly without forming some kind of link – however tenuous. Often a nod leads to chat and then to a discovery of common interests.

Pets are known to help people to work through the stages of grief following bereavement. They provide a sense of being needed and a source of living touch. Affectionate cats who sleep on laps promote a sense of peace and well-being and do fulfil, to some extent, the basic biological need for regular contact with some other living thing. Some owners believe that they have a high level of communication with animals, to whom they attribute many human characteristics.

But there is a cost to everything, and you must remember that pets have short lives and that, if you become too devoted, you may have to go through another bereavement.

## Smoking and Drinking

These can be dismissed quickly. Smoking is an evil on every count and the first priority in the life of any person who smokes is to stop. There is no need for me to emphasise the dangers – everyone knows that smoking is a menace to health. But not everyone knows that smoking is one of the chief risk factors for sudden death from a heart attack and is regularly a cause of angina pectoris, coronary thrombosis, severe disablement from disease of the arteries supplying blood to the legs and from what is called obstructive airway disease.

Smoking is one of the causes of atherosclerosis – an artery disease leading to narrowing and obstruction – and this, in turn, leads to all sorts of unpleasantness. The direct effect on the lungs – quite apart from the cancer risk – is to encourage emphysema and chronic bronchitis and progressively to reduce the efficiency of the respiratory system. Truly, the plight of the respiratory cripple is dreadful – constant exhausting, laboured breathing, even at rest in bed, the lips blue and the shoulders heaving in the fight to get enough air, no prospect for progressive deterioration. This is what smoking and neglect of chest infection can do.

The way to stop smoking is to stop. Right now, in the middle of a packet. Plenty of ordinary people have done it and have been surprised at how easy it was. I speak from personal experience. Don't make a fuss about it. Don't play for sympathy. Forget the stories about tobacco addiction – this is a myth fostered by people looking for an excuse to continue. Forget the idea that you can cut down gradually. Forget the gadgets and hypnotism, and the evening classes in giving up. All these are simply ways of putting off the crunch. They just mean that you're not serious.

Alcohol is a real blessing but is easily abused, especially by the lonely and socially deprived. Many bereaved people fall quickly into habits of over-indulgence, perhaps feeling justified by depression and insomnia. The risks are addiction, liver damage, pancreatitis and, eventually, after a long time, brain damage. Women are especially susceptible. Just look out for the danger signs:

Thinking a lot about alcohol.

Forming regular patterns of taking more than one drink.

Drinking early in the day, or regularly at lunch-time.

Alcohol beginning to interfere with normal activities.

Regular need for larger quantities.

Feeling physically bad every morning.

Don't worry about regular moderate drinking. A daily habit doesn't mean that you are in danger. Just watch the quantities. Estimate your intake in units. A unit is a measure of spirit, a glass of wine or a half-pint of beer. Exceed five units a day, every day, and you are likely to do yourself a physical injury. This is not to suggest that a maximum of five units a day is necessarily a safe level of drinking – susceptibility to alcohol damage varies considerably from person to person – but you would be unlucky if it did harm you.

## Health Danger Signs

There are some warnings which older people should never disregard and which should be taken as an indication for an immediate visit to a doctor. Look out for:

Unexplained loss of weight.

A cough which does not settle in two or three weeks.

Any *new* signs of indigestion.

A new and persistent pain in the chest or abdomen.

Any obvious and persistent alteration in the bowel habits.

Black stools.

A new lump in the breast or a new lump anywhere else.

Menstrual-type bleeding after the menopause.

A new tendency to accidents.

None of these need necessarily mean that something serious is going on, but any of them could, and it would be just plain foolishness to ignore any of these important indications.

Finally, try to analyse whether there are any health risk factors which were being kept in check by the person who has died. Some of these are obvious – such as advice on weight control, exercise, worrying, and so on. But others may be less obvious. Remember, for instance, that you may, before you were bereaved, have been spared dangerous activities in the home – climbing ladders, doing electrical repairs, carrying awkward loads on steep stairs, and so on. Accidents in the home are a *very* common cause of serious and painful disability, and now that you are on your own, you are likely to be more liable to them. You cannot be too careful.

# 12 Rebuilding Your Life

## RESTRUCTURING LIFE

By now you will be clearly aware of the principle that time, by itself, heals nothing. Only living, experiencing, working, relating, can fill the gap left by the loss of your former partner. The worst thing possible is just to sit around and bemoan your fate. That simply wastes time – most of us have little enough of that left. Like computers, human beings need programming – software that brings them to life, makes them capable of great things. When you lost your loved one, a large part of the programming that was then appropriate, ceased to be relevant to your continuing life. You need – you *must* have – new input, new software in the form of new experience. And that experience must be direct experience of other people.

People vary considerably in the degree to which they need others. Some are remarkably self-sufficient and seem to be able, quite happily, to lead solitary lives, emphasising the distinction between loneliness and being alone. But none of us can live even reasonably full lives without human associations. The lives of the hermits, the recluses, are always stunted, defective, often very unhappy. This is because they do not get the kind of input necessary for full living. They just go on using the same narrow, self-regarding programme, and if they change, it is likely to be a change for the worse.

You are likely, at first, to resist the urging to meet new people, make new friends, even, perhaps, move in with someone new. You will probably feel that this would involve infidelity to the old partner – that you are dropping the standards you have maintained for so long. This is understandable but illogical and wrong. Apart from some areas where male chauvinism has insisted on wives remaining unmarried after the death of the husband, society has always accepted the rights of bereaved people to seek new partners. This acceptance is based on a clear realisation that the needs of the living must take precedence over the, probably imaginary, rights of the dead. It is interesting that, even in those communities or groups professing to believe in the immortality of the soul and the eventual re-uniting with the deceased, there is no objection to re-marriage, after the lapse of a reasonable time. I regard this as a triumph of common sense and human need over superstition.

You do, of course, have a choice. You can cut yourself off from all human intercourse, dedicating yourself to the memory of the deceased and let your life stop at the point of your bereavement. Or you can, while preserving your cherished memories of, and respect for, the life which was lived and is now ended, decided that your own life *is* going to go on. This is the correct, the courageous choice. Bereavement, ironically, can be an opportunity for you. Many, relieved of marital and other responsibilities, have found that they are able to break out of a comfortable but unprofitable rut, into a new and more rewarding way of life.

## Making New Friends

You must go about this in a positive and systematic way. I am talking about deliberately putting yourself in the way of people who can be important in your life, either directly, as close associates, or indirectly for what they can give you in the way of mental stimulation and encouragement to action. Age has nothing to do with it, neither has physical condition. There are plenty of people around older and physically worse off than you, and if you go about it the right way, you may be surprised at the splash you make.

Making new friends and acquaintances will take some effort on your part, but this need involve little more than registering for one or two evening classes at your local Adult Education Centre, joining a club, getting in touch, by advertisement if necessary, with people with whom you can share joint hobby activities, perhaps even using a computer match-making agency. Go and speak to the librarian at your Public Library and find out what is available.

Establishing new interest is almost as important as meeting new people and the one, of course, tends to lead to the other. Continuing education is very much a part of the process. Don't be put off by recollection of unfortunate educational experiences you may have had earlier in life. Adult education has never been livelier or more accessible. Many courses, covering a vast range of subjects, are now available and are usually structured for those who have never had the chance to engage in the broader aspects of education. Experience has shown that people with very little formal education – often quite elderly people – can take great benefit from studying subjects like sociology, psychology, philosophy, current affairs, history, literature and science. You never know what you can do until you try – painting, sculpture, writing, counselling, yoga, public speaking, teaching.

You are probably past your first flush of life, and you may think that you are too old for this sort of thing. That is nonsense. You have many qualifications, from your life experience, that are not possessed by the young. You are likely to have much to contribute, in a circle of people, of all ages, many of them perhaps less well-motivated than you are.

Perhaps you think you are too old to learn. Well, the popular view, about not being able to teach an old dog new tricks, may apply to old dogs, but it certainly doesn't apply to old people. Only the completely demented have lost all capacity for learning and if those of us who are not demented fail to learn, it is because we don't try. In fact, we are all of us learning, all the time. If we did not, life would be impossible. The real question is – *how much* are we learning? There is plenty of clear evidence that none of us makes use of more than a small fraction of our potential brain power. This is to some extent due to the deplorable cultural attitudes of society which take it for granted that the elderly are useless.

Well I, for one, know a number of old people whose current contribution to society is many times greater than that of thousands of young people – old people who learned more after the age of fifty than most learn in a lifetime. There is nothing remarkable about this. It is simply a matter of motivation – of being determined not to conform sheepishly to the stereotype, and of trying to make as much of one's life as possible.

The convention of retirement into idleness and futility is a social and personal disaster and a sure prescription for an early death. It may have something to do with the unpleasantness which characterised the working life of so many in the past – physically over-burdened labourers who spent their time dreaming of the day when they could stop. But work *is* life, as many are now beginning to understand and your object should not be to avoid it, but to make it as rewarding and congenial as possible. Without work, the body and the mind begin to deteriorate.

## Continuing Sexual Life?

Bereavement has many facets and, to some, the loss of the sexual life is one of the hardest to bear. Happy and satisfying sex with a good partner implies much more than 'sexual technique'. It implies an underlying loving relationship of which sex is the most eloquent expression. To lose such a relationship is indeed hard to bear. Many feel that such loss cannot be remedied, that after losing such a partner one must simply resign oneself to a celibate life.

Certainly it is a mistake to rush into promiscuity. This is not uncommon following bereavement, and the results are predictably painful. Sex can never be a satisfactory end in itself, and the attempt to use it in this way – to trade the temporary excitements of variety for the proper use of a precious commodity – has been found by millions to bring nothing but grief. Because sex is the ultimate vehicle for the expression of love, it is always liable to be interpreted, by the recipient, as being an expression of love. If it is not, the result is havoc. Millions, of both sexes, have suffered painfully, in their feelings and emotions, from the depredations of the cold-heartedly promiscuous.

Bereavement is no excuse for such conduct. But neither is it a reason to write off the rest of your life in celibacy. First you must work out your grief, and the time this takes will vary greatly from case to case – perhaps a year, perhaps longer. Then you must find a partner available and worthy of you. Such a person certainly exists – not one, but many. You may be sure that there are thousands in your situation, each one longing to meet someone like you. But you will not meet by sitting at home hoping for a ring on the doorbell. You have to do something about it, as I have already suggested.

## A Miracle

One must never give up hope. Abundant life can grow out of an adversity even as great as bereavement. This book has been much concerned with death, but it is essentially a book about life and about hope. Here, to end, is the story of Peter Dunbar and Marlene Weiss – a story of renewal and the triumph of life.

Peter was a fastidious man and, at first, the thought of Marlene's wheel-chair life, with its degrading dependence, filled him with distaste. But as his delight in their conversation grew it came to concern him less and less. They had met at a weekly music appreciation group and, as time passed, he found he was looking forward with ever-growing interest to Friday evenings. He was a successful chemical engineer, a widower of forty-seven, who, after nineteen years of an excellent marriage, had been cruelly bereaved three years before when his wife had contracted Ebola virus haemorrhagic fever while on a visit to West Africa. In a desperate quest for consolation, Peter had engaged in a succession of disastrous affairs which had left him desperate, humiliated and impotent.

Marlene, a cultivated, intelligent and sensitive woman in her late thirties, had also suffered. She had had a violently passionate relationship with a man whose ungovernable sexual sadism and brutality had become apparent only after they were married. Her pride and refusal to face the full enormity of the situation had forced her to stay with him until, in the end, his assaults had culminated in a terrible beating in which a violent blow to her spine had deprived her of the use of her legs. Her husband had been arrested and had served a prison sentence, during which she had divorced him. She had never seen him again and, when she left hospital, had gone to live with a sister, who attended to all her needs.

Music had been a consolation to her, as she strove to come to terms with her new situation and she had taken up, once again, the study of the flute. Her progress had been rapid, and with the new insights of maturity, had acquired, in the course of a few months, a control of technique that freed her interpretive spirit to reach levels of musicality that surprised her.

Peter felt that she was of a quality far beyond his reach. For years he had believed himself a failure in all the arts of human communication and he attributed the apparent ease and pleasantness of their discourse solely to her tact and kindness.

In the course of their conversations she had, inevitably, referred to her special musical interests. Without telling her, he had gone to Foyles and bought some music for flute and piano, including three sonatas by Bach, and had begun to practice the piano parts. Three weeks later, feeling himself ready, he said, with carefully assumed casualness:
'... like the ritenuto at the end of the Siciliano ...'

She looked at him sharply. 'You mean Bach's E flat ...?'

'Yes.'

The corners of her mouth twitched. 'Exactly!' she said, 'Can you play it?'

But the implications deterred him from immediately inviting her to play with him.

In the event, his fears were groundless. Precisely at the time agreed, she drew up in her narrow little hand-controlled car and parked neatly just outside his house. Her light-weight, folding wheel-chair was stowed behind her seat and he soon had it out and set up. Then, with matter-of-fact neutrality, she said, 'Let me put my arm round your neck.' In a moment she had slipped gracefully into her chair. The contact was brief, physically intimate but impersonal.

The evening was a success beyond his expectations and they played for two hours, unaware of the passage of time. He was amazed at her technique and musical sensitivity and delighted to find a rapport that almost made words unnecessary. She was a far better musician than he, but he played better than he had ever done. The Bach sonatas, in particular, went so well that, when they finished, they sat smiling at each other. There was such a strong sense of communication that he knew that their relationship had moved into a new phase. By tacit consent, they stopped, and she began to dismantle and dry her instrument.

'I must go in half an hour.' she said.

And so was established the pattern of the weeks that followed. At first the performance of music remained the primary purpose, but gradually the pleasure in music-making gave way to an equal satisfaction in the subsequent conversations. She was unusually well-read and their talk ranged over a wide field – literature, art, philosophy, music, politics. In a spirit of friendly competitiveness, he would deliberately introduce abstruse allusions and, with much laughter, she would respond with equally arcane references. The prevailing mood was one of perfect security; for him, through her physical helplessness and passivity, and, for her, through his gentleness, unassertive kindness and the conviction that he posed no physical threat.

In this climate of confidence he was able to contemplate discussing with her the sexual problems that had humiliated him, belittling his own image of himself and twisting his every human contact. And so, one evening, when they had played a Faure piece and Gluck's *Dance of the Blessed Spirits* he allowed his appreciation of her playing to modulate into an acknowledgement of her friendship and the reason it meant so much to him.

Her response was so sensitively understanding and encouraging that he found himself, almost with volition, talking about his bereavement, about the dreadful emptiness it had left in his life, about the fiascos that had followed, and, to his astonishment, about his impotence. She listened with grave attention, saying nothing, but merely smiling sadly. When he was finished, she said, 'These women seem to you to have treated you very badly, but you were probably looking for something they could never give you. You just wanted your wife all over again. As for the last one, Jane ... well, I don't think people tear at one another without reasons that seem good to them. The aggressors, too, are the victims ...'

Then, with calm lack of emphasis and avoidance of censure, she told him the story of her own injury. 'According to the neurosurgeon' she concluded, with a wry smile, 'I made a complete recovery from the organic injury to the spinal cord. So I supposed it's all in the mind. Unfortunately, that's not much consolation ...'

The weeks passed and spring gave way to a radiant summer and with the change came a commensurate flowering of their feelings and a deepening mutual involvement. One day, anxious to share with her a further facet of pleasure, he suggested that he should take her, the following Sunday, to see a place he had loved from boyhood. After only a moment's hesitation, she agreed.

He was not heedless of the practical consequences of inviting her to spend several hours alone in his company, and when he hinted at these, she laughed and said, 'Amor vincit omnia! I take it as a compliment that you are so anxious to be with me, that you have overcome your delicacy in such matters!'

Her use of the Latin tag, with its casual implication, amazed and delighted him. But it also reminded him that her deepest wound related to a crisis of failure in human love and that her most central quality was the protective chastity that had necessarily followed. And he wondered what kind of love it was to which she so carelessly referred.

She was sitting in her wheel-chair when he arrived and her sister, a cheerful older woman whom he liked on sight, pushed her out to his car and helped her in. The chair was folded and stowed in the back and they set off in high spirits. He had noted at once that, instead of her usual slacks, she was wearing a short, light summer dress, without tights, and, as they drove along his curiosity compelled the occasional quick glance at her legs. At length she could contain neither amusement nor comment.

'How unimaginative of me,' she said, smiling broadly, 'not to realise that you would naturally expect my legs to be wasted and horrid. Well I'm pleased to say they're not. You don't have to be so furtive.' She pulled up her dress. 'I don't mind you looking at them, since that's all they're good for.' There was no bitterness in her tone, but to emphasise her lack of resentment she playfully ruffled his hair.

They drove to a spot with a superb view which it would be impossible to reach in a wheelchair, for the last thirty yards or so involved a narrow stony path through a small copse of trees. But he wanted to carry her and to show her that he could. So, after pushing the chair for a quarter of a mile from where he had parked the car, he shouldered the small rucksack containing the sandwiches and the beer cans and said, 'This is where we park the chair.'

She looked at him in mock alarm. 'I hope it's not too far!'

Peter acquitted himself well, and although more than a little breathless when they reached their destination, was able to put her down gently in a grassy hollow at the edge of the trees, and had enough energy left to hurry back to fold away the chair and hide it behind some bushes. When he returned, she was sitting up gazing around at the splendid panorama below them. She looked up when he appeared and with a cry of 'How lovely!' stretched out her hand to him.

He sat down beside her and for a few minutes they remained silent, enjoying the privacy and proximity in a place of such beauty. At length she said, 'I don't know how well I managed to conceal that I was quite dead inside. But I want you to know that you have brought me back to life.' And with that she put her arms round his neck and lay back, drawing him to her.

He kissed her and she held his head to keep his mouth on hers. As she did so, he found, to his astonishment, that a power that had been absent for years was restored to him. At the same time, she, too, knew what had happened and he felt her mouth curving under his in a smile. She pulled his head back gently and said, 'Oh darling! How wonderful!' Then, with her lips brushing his, she added urgently, 'Don't waste it! Go on! Quickly!'

He found her very ready and it was soon over. For a long time they lay close, then some intuition caused him to move away a little so that he could look at her face. There were tears on her cheeks, and he was arrested by an extraordinary expression which seemed compounded of love, amazement and exultation.

'What is it?' he asked, 'What's happening?'

She opened her eyes and looked at him with concentrated intentness. Then the tension relaxed and she sat up, pulled down her dress, and smiled. 'It's a question of priority,' she said, 'Whether to tell you that I love you, or that *I can walk!*'

# Books of Interest

*Dying* John Hinton (Pelican Books, 1972)
*On Death and Dying Elizabeth Kubler-Ross* (Tavistock Publications 1969)
*The Way We Die* Leslie Ivan and Maureen Melrose (Angel Press, 1986)
*Living with Death and Dying* Elizabeth Kubler-Ross (Souvenir, 1982)
*On Children and Death* Elizabeth Kubler-Ross (Collier Macmillan, 1984)
Cicely Saunders: The Founder of the Hospice Movement Shirley du Boulay (Hodder & Stoughton, 1984)
*The Hospice Way* Denise Winn (Macdonald Optima, 1987)
*The Hospice Alternative* Margaret Manning (Souvenir, 1984)
*Bereavement: Studies of Grief in Adult Life* Colin Murray Parkes (Pelican Books, 1986)
*Recovery from Bereavement* Colin Murray Parkes and Robert E. Weiss (Harper & Row, 1983)
*Readings in Aging and Death* Ed: Steven H. Zarit (Harper and Row, 1977)
*Living with Loss* Liz McNeill Taylor (Fontana Paperbacks, 1983)
*Survival Guide for Widows* June Hemer and Ann Stanyer (Age Concern, 1986)
*Counseling the Dying* Margaretta K. Bowers, Edgar N. Jackson, James A. Knight and Lawrence LeShan (Jason Aronson, New York, 1986)
*Care of the Dying* Richard Lamerton (Pelican Books)
*Mourning and Melancholia* Sigmund Freud (Hogarth Press, 1951)
*Miracles of Courage* Monica Dickens (David & Charles, 1987)
*Brief Lives* Living with the Death of a Child S. Foster and P. Smith (Arlington, 1987)
*The Courage to Grieve* Judy Tatelbaum (Cedar Books, 1986)
*Death and the Family* Lily Pincus (Faber & Faber, 1976)
*Living with Grief* Tony Lake (Sheldon Press, 1984)
*When Bad things Happen* to Good People Harold Kushner (Pan Books, 1982)
*Letting Go* Ian Ainsworth-Smith and Peter Speck (SPCK, 1982)

*Don't Take My Grief Away* Doug Manning (Harper & Row, 1985)
*The Bereaved Parent* Harriet Sarnoff Schiff (Souvenir Press, 1985)
*How it Feels When a Parent Dies* Jill Krementz (Gollancz, 1983)
*A Very Easy Death* Jessica Mitford (Hutchinson, 1963)
*The Loved One: An American Tragedy* Evelyn Waugh (Chapman & Hall, 1949)
*Stress, Loss and Grief* John Schneider (University Park Press, Baltimore, 1984)
*Loss – An Invitation to Grow* Jean C. Grigor (Arthur James, 1986)
*I Can't Face Tomorrow* Norman Keir (Thorsons, 1986)
*Through Grief – The Bereavement Journey* Elizabeth Collick (Darton, Longman & Todd/CRUSE, 1986)
*A Child Dies* J.H. Arnold & P.B. Gemma (Aspen Publications, 1983)
*Facing Death* Averil Stedeford (Heinemann, 1984)
*Grief Counselling and Grief Therapy* J.W. Worden (Tavistock Publications, 1983)
*Take Care of your Elderly Relative* Muir Gray and Heather McKenzie (Allen & Unwin, 1980)
*Taking Over* Avril Rodway (Columbus Books, 1987)
*Aging and the Human Condition* Ed: Gari Lesnoff-Caravaglia (Human Sciences Press, 1982)
*Ageing:* The Biology of Senescence Alex Comfort (Routledge & Kegan Paul, 1964)
*All in the End is Harvest* An anthology for those who grieve Ed: Anhes Whitaker (Darton, Longman and Todd, 1984)

# Index